A NEW DAWN RISING
"Rethinking Christian Struggles"

By: Dr. Delron Shirley

© 2018

This teaching manual is intended for personal study; however, the author encourages all students to also become teachers and to share the truths from this text with others. However, copying the text itself without permission from the author is considered plagiarism, which is punishable by law. To obtain permission to quote material from this book, please contact:

Delron Shirley
3210 Cathedral Spires Dr.
Colorado Springs, CO 80904
www.teachallnationsmission.com
teachallnations@msn.com

Table of Contents

Preface 4
Passion in a Parked Car 5
Travailing in Prayer 13
The Prayer of Importunity.. 27
Wrestling with Principalities 39
More Than Conquerors.. 51
Kingdom Violence... 59
The Armor of God 71
The Weapons of Our Warfare...................................... 83
The Ultimate Example... 103
Teach All Nations Mission.. 111
Books by Delron & Peggy Shirley 113

Preface

This volume is part of a trilogy of short independent works that are intended to stand alone but should also be read as a series since they have a unifying theme. Good People, Bad Things, and Vice Versa deals with the age-old question of why God allows bad things to happen to good people and good things to happen to bad people; the sequel, A New Dawn Rises, deals with the struggles that we go through as Christians, and the concluding volume, Becoming a Person of Legacy, suggests an approach to living a life that makes a lasting mark in history. The consistent thread that is woven throughout the fiber of each book is the biblical principle that a man is what he thinks about in his heart (Proverbs 23:7) and that we have to determine not to be forced into the mold of thinking like everyone else does (Romans 12:2) – hence, the tile: The Non-Conformer's Trilogy.

Passion in a Parked Car

As it sat in the parking lot of Bragaw Dormitory on the campus of North Carolina State University that frosty fall night, the windows of my 1969 Mustang were totally fogged up from the heavy breathing of the passionate activity inside the flashy coupe. But I have to go back and tell the backstory that leads up to this evening before we open the door to the little sports car and expose what's going on inside.

You see, I grew up in a very strict Pentecostal environment where we were taught that to be friends with world made you an enemy of God. (James 4:4) In fact, we were so strict about not associating with "the world" that we were almost afraid to be too friendly with Methodist, Baptists, and Presbyterians. For certain, we would never even think of becoming friends with Episcopalians or Catholics. But now that I was away in college, I was developing friendships with other students who were not only those "questionable" Presbyterians and Episcopalians – also with some students who drank, steamed up the windshields of their cars on a regular basis, smoked pot, experimented with LSD, and who knows what else. This was quite a challenge for someone who had grown up with the motto, "We don't smoke, drink, or chew – or run with them that do"!

I guess you could say that the mantra of my church leaders was, "Holiness without which no man will see God." (Hebrews 12:14) Our strict code of modesty ruled that our girls wear skirts for physical education class rather than the school-issued gym shorts. Of course, there were plenty of regulations that had to do with hair and make-up – taboos that kept the women so "unpretentious" (okay, let's be honest – so ugly) that it's a wonder they ever got married. But now that I was away from home I had developed friendships with classmates who broke all those rules. Well, actually, they weren't technically breaking any rules because they didn't grow up under such restrictions. Nonetheless, I found myself running with a crowd that I would have never envisioned before.

    Although it was never said in so many words, I could always know what was acceptable and unacceptable behavior by one simple test: "If it's fun, it's sin." I remember not being permitted to eat at a popular pizza shop because they served beer. Even though no one at our table would be drinking, the fact that there would be alcohol on the premises made the establishment off limits to our church leadership.

    Of course, we lived by a very regimented observance of religious duties. For instance, we honored the Sabbath Day by never doing any form of work – not even washing clothes on Sunday. I remember one weekend when my mother needed some clothes cleaned for Monday morning, so she stayed up past midnight to use the washing machine – when the only work she was going to do was tossing the clothes into the machine and taking them out to transfer them to the dryer. Another example was our dutiful tithing. I remember hearing one man testify about how his car broke down on the week he had failed to pay his tithes, costing him the same amount of money that he would have given to the church had he paid his tithes. He concluded with, "So, God got His tithes anyway." I remember – even though I was just a young child – thinking that there was something wrong with that picture. Unless God was running the local auto garage, I could not connect the repair bill with the man's tithing. Looking back on that incident some sixty years later, my reaction today is, "Those were the good old days – when you could get your car repaired for one tenth of a week's wage!"

Let me wrap up my ruminations about my upbringing by recalling one particular sermon in which the pastor was trying to encourage the members to be faithful in their church attendance by being present every time the church doors were open. He waxed eloquent in describing how many temptations and struggles were waiting in the outside world to ensnare us and said that we could never get enough of what it takes to resist the world, the flesh, and the devil in just one service on Sunday morning. Definitely we needed that extra dose from the Sunday night service. And, by the time we had rubbed shoulders with the world for the first three days of the week, we needed the "booster shot" of the midweek service in order to make it through to the next Sunday.

This brings us back to the steamed up windows in my Mustang. I hate to disappoint you, but the passionate activity in the front seat wasn't the "making out" with my girlfriend that you've probably been imagining for the past several paragraphs. It was a passionate hours-long prayer struggle. I had wanted a private place to do some deep soul searching, and the only place that I knew I could be totally alone would be in my car away from all the other campus activity. That night, I wanted to settle a deeply troubling heart-level question, "Was there something wrong with me? Was I not a real Christian?" Because I didn't find the Christian life to be a constant struggle as all the preachers in my life had always said, I was afraid that I was missing something. After all, I was friends with "the world," and that must make me an enemy of God. Yes, I understood that my friends who slept around and used drugs were plain and simple sinners, but I was questioning why I didn't see anything wrong with my friends who claimed to be Christians even though they didn't comply with all the rules and regulations that I had always been taught were obligatory. I couldn't help questioning if I had somehow deceived myself into believing that I was okay because I didn't find my life to be an uphill struggle. Perhaps, I was the dead fish that I had heard so many sermons about – the one who was floating downstream while all the live fish were busily swimming upstream against the current.

That night in my little sports car with the steamed-up windows, I finally came to some powerful realizations. I understood something about the whole "holiness without which no man shall see God" teaching. I realized that Jesus had given us another avenue for seeing God – to have a pure heart. (Matthew 5:8) I also realized that He had given us another approach to fulfilling all the laws and requirements of God – living in love rather than trying to count the pennies in our tithing or monitoring what is being served at the other tables in the restaurants we are eating in, or even calling in the "modesty police" every time we get dressed. (Mark 12:30-31)

Reflecting back on the grappling of that night in the dorm parking lot, I can see one significant component in my life that got me to that place. And, amazingly, that very same aspect of my life is what took me through the struggle and out the other side. That astonishing element was my relationship with my parents. Because I had seen my parents continually demonstrating sacrificial love for me, I had grown up with a deep-seated love and respect for them. My father worked two jobs in order to supply for his family – a comfortable home, nice clothes so that we never felt awkward in school, fun vacations so we could grow up with happy family memories, and a college fund to ensure that we would have the very best opportunities for a making our own future. In fact, when I was applying for college during my senior year in high school, I received less-substantial scholarship offers than some of my classmates who were less academically qualified. The explanation that the scholarship committee gave me was that my father had saved up too much money in my scholarship fund. The irony is that he actually made less money that my classmates' fathers. He had just lived sacrificially in order to provide for me. My mother and father lived very sacrificially – bypassing things that they wanted for themselves, going to work when they physically were not able, and generally pinching every penny so they could see that their children not only didn't lack anything as we were growing up but also so that we had sufficient for our futures. As I observed this kind of selfless love from them, I developed a heart relationship in which I never wanted to disappoint or disobey them. I wasn't afraid of breaking their rules; I was afraid of breaking their hearts.

Because I had learned to see life through the eyes of that kind of love, I was not struggling with "the world" because I was not drawn to participate in its temptations even though I was constantly surrounded by them. So, it was because of growing up in this sacrificially loving environment that I was drawn to the place of a disconnect between my life experience and the religious ideology that I had accepted. That night in the front seat of my car, I realized that true Christianity is exactly the same – it's not about breaking the rules of our Heavenly Father, but about breaking His heart. The Father so loved us that He gave His own Son for us, and Jesus so loved us that He gave His own life for us. When we really realize what that love is all about, the rules become insignificant in comparison to our desire to honor such a heart of love! Likewise, it was the sacrificially loving environment of my parents' home that gave me the background to walk away from this struggle triumphantly.

Many years later, my teenage son was in a discipleship program that required that the father and son do certain exercises together each week. As I was reading the manual, I began to see that much of the training was based on an obedience model in which the son was taught to obey – and essentially fear – the father. I challenged the leader of the discipleship program about the material, telling him that the teaching was flawed in that it presented an erroneous image of God. He responded by telling me about how his father demanded obedience and punished disobedience. The result was the nice, disciplined man that he had grown up to be. I countered with the story of how my father had been so sacrificially loving and told him that the result was that I saw the true nature of God in him and then learned to relate to God out of loving respect rather than judgmental fear. The gentleman's response was, "Well, you're probably the only person I know who feels that way!" I don't think that I was ever able to get through to this poor misinformed, misdirected, and just plain mistaken mentor that he was taking the totally wrong approach. By teaching young men to esteem their parents through a fearful respect for their position of authority, he was causing them to develop a distorted view of their Heavenly Father. Certainly, most fathers today lack the sacrificial love that my parents excelled in; however, I'm certain that almost every child can find at least one example of this kind of love in his parents. By helping his students focus on such instances and magnify them in their heart, the mentor could have helped change the relationships between the young men and women in his program and their earthly fathers – and their Heavenly Father. In doing so, he could have been part of the answer by bringing the promised restoration of the home prophesied in Malachi 4:6 rather than being part of the problem by perpetuating the curse of broken family relationships also prophesied in this concluding verse of the Old Testament.

And he shall turn the heart of the fathers to the children, and the heart of the children to their fathers, lest I come and smite the earth with a curse.

The point of this story is that many times – if not most of the time – we Christians find ourselves fighting the wrong battles against the wrong enemies with the wrong weapons. Behind that fogged-up windshield, I realized that I didn't have to struggle against the world, the flesh, and the devil – constantly needing a "booster shot" to make it. I needed to struggle against the false ideas that were trying to mold my image of God and my relationship with Him into a distorted, flawed, and dangerous picture. My enemy was a wrong conception of the way that I am to relate to God – not my relationship with the "world."

When we really get the right perspective on things we'll discover that our struggles are not so much against external forces contending <u>against</u> us but against our own misconceptions and dysfunctional ideas that are contending <u>within</u> us.

Travailing in Prayer

Now that I've introduced you to my agonizing night of prayer in that dormitory parking lot, I guess that the best place for me to begin our journey would be with the idea of travailing in prayer. The concept of travailing in prayer comes from a couple statements in the writings of the Apostle Paul, "My little children, of whom I travail in birth again until Christ be formed in you" (Galatians 4:19) and "Neither did we eat any man's bread for nought; but wrought with labour and travail night and day, that we might not be chargeable to any of you" (II Thessalonians 3:8).

Interestingly, neither of these verses actually speak of prayer in relationship to the travailing that the apostle acknowledged as part of his life and ministry.

The Thessalonian passage is clearly in the context of physical work in that he makes repeated reference to manual labor as he furthers the discussion of the topic all the way through verse fifteen – demanding that the people within the church follow his example of earning their own way through manual employment. In setting the bar for others to conquer, Paul stressed that the work he did was not just light chores but such intensive exertion that it could literally be labeled as "travail." Of course, we must remember that Paul may also have been dealing with some lingering disabilities from having been stoned to the point that he was either dead or so so close to death that the murderous mob thought that they had achieved their goal. Even though he was raised back to life and courageously took on a sixty-mile journey – possibly on foot – the very next day, we have no record as to whether there were residual impairments that would have made manual labor difficult and painful for the apostle.

In the passage from Galatians, Paul is talking about ministering the Word. The entire context of the chapter is about helping mature the believers from spiritual childhood where they think like slaves to spiritual sonship where they be able to think like heirs of the promises and provisions of God. Notice that in verse eleven Paul declares that he bestows labor into this endeavor, which he defines in verse thirteen as preaching with the objective that he describes in verse sixteen as telling them the truth. As a writer and a teacher, I can totally understand what the apostle was trying to communicate in this passage. Expressing the truth in a way that it can effectively impact people is genuinely hard work – travail, if you please. The audience who hears a sermon or lesson or who reads a book or article has no idea how much has gone into the research and presentation of the message. There are no records kept of the times that that each sentence is written, deleted, and rephrased. It would be impossible to calculate the number of time that the author, pastor, or teacher has had to stop writing and just rest his head in his hands while trying to find the right illustration to make the message come alive. No one knows the times that he has to resort to the dictionary or thesaurus to try to find exactly the right word to express his thought. Mark Twain once said that the difference between the right word and almost the right word is the difference between lightning and a lightning bug. As a minster who knew that it would take lightning rather than lightning bugs to get his audience from spiritual slavery to mature sonship, Paul literally travailed as he penned the words of his epistles. When writing to his prime disciple, Paul reiterated that ministering the Word of God and correct doctrine is actually a form of labor or hard work. (I Timothy 5:17)

    Now, back to the contemporary idea of travailing in prayer. Just because Paul might not have been talking about prayer when he spoke of travailing in these two verses, does this negate the whole idea? After all, Paul did ask the Christians in Rome to strive together with him in their prayers to God (Romans 15:30); so, there must be a place for confrontational spiritual prayer.

Let me address this issue by analyzing one of the biblical illustrations commonly referenced to bolster the idea – the story of Jacob's wresting match with an angel.

> And Jacob was left alone; and there wrestled a man with him until the breaking of the day. And when he saw that he prevailed not against him, he touched the hollow of his thigh; and the hollow of Jacob's thigh was out of joint, as he wrestled with him. And he said, Let me go, for the day breaketh. And he said, I will not let thee go, except thou bless me. And he said unto him, What is thy name? And he said, Jacob. And he said, Thy name shall be called no more Jacob, but Israel: for as a prince hast thou power with God and with men, and hast prevailed. And Jacob asked him, and said, Tell me, I pray thee, thy name. And he said, Wherefore is it that thou dost ask after my name? And he blessed him there. And Jacob called the name of the place Peniel: for I have seen God face to face, and my life is preserved. (Genesis 32:24-30)

There are a number of significant elements that must be understood before this passage takes on the life that God intended for it to have. The most important aspect is the context in which this struggle took place. Jacob was on his way back to his homeland – a country that he had abandoned after cheating his brother out of his inheritance. (Genesis 27:1-28:2) As he fled from the land that had been given to his family by a divine covenant through his grandfather (Genesis 12:1), God Himself appeared to Jacob and confirmed to him that He would be with him as he went out of the land and that He would bring him back to the land he was fleeing and give it to him. He went on to assure Jacob that He would not leave him until all the words of His promise had been fulfilled. Additionally, He extended the covenant that He had given to Abraham to Jacob with the promise of the proliferation of his descendants and the multiplication of their influence among all the families of the world. (Genesis 28:13-15) After an extended stay in the home of his uncle/father-in-law Laban, the day came when God again spoke to Jacob, telling him to return to the land of his father and grandfather – ultimately, his own land. (Genesis 31:3) With that command came a promise from the very lips of God Himself, "I will be with thee."

We see that the backstory to this episode in Jacob's life was God's repeated guarantee of protection and promise of possession of the covenant land. It is of utmost significance that we bear this in mind when we read the story of how Jacob strategized the meeting with the brother with whom he had so treacherously dealt. He sent out two convoys of camels, sheep, goats, cattle, and servants followed by his family. Finally, he lagged behind – leaving himself space to escape just in case the brother was not appeased by the gifts and slaughtered his wives and children. All this scheming was diligently covered with prayer and intercession that God would somehow grant him favor and calm Esau's thirst for revenge. It was into this anxious environment that the angel entered and Jacob challenged him to a dual.

With the understanding that Jacob had been promised time and again that God was to take him back safely to the land of his father, the whole process of sending gifts (actually, bribes) to his brother and the strategy of hiding behind his wives and children seems totally pointless – as does the struggle with the angel. Essentially, all these schemes were nothing more than a demonstration of his lack of faith in the promises of God. Had Jacob been a man of faith like his grandfather, he would have welcomed the angelic guest with reverence and respect as Abraham did when he was visited by the angelic messengers in the plains of Mamre. (Genesis 18:1-8)

Even more intriguing is the fact that the angelic wresting match was not the only supernatural encounter that Jacob had in this experience. He was also visited by angels in the first verse of the chapter, but the biblical record does not indicate that Jacob received any kind of encouragement or direction through the divine encounter. Like many who encountered the supernatural miracles in the life of Jesus and yet refused to accept that He was truly the Son of God, Jacob acknowledged that the host of God had appeared to him but named the place Mahanaim (Two Camps) – signifying that he was going forward with his own scheme of sending two envoys to Esau rather than asking for God's direction in this moment of crisis.

Then, after initiating his plan, Jacob chose to wrestle with – rather than to ask for divine council from – the angel who continued with him. As day was breaking, the angel conceded that he was not able to subdue Jacob and had to cripple him in order to end the struggle. Even though it may seem that Jacob actually won the contest, we must remember that he limped away from the wresting match with a disability that plagued him the rest of his life. The New Testament account is careful to point out that he was still dependent upon his crutch on the day he died – an ongoing consequence of the struggle of his stubborn will against the messenger of God. (Hebrews 11:21)

The one aspect of this wrestling match that makes it seem that Jacob was actually the winner was his insistence that he would not let his opponent go until he blessed him. In fact, the blessing that the angel pronounced over him that daybreak actually included the declaration that Jacob had prevailed. (Genesis 32:28) Before we jump to any conclusions, let's take a trip back through the background that led up to this event. It all started with Jacob's decision to go along with his mother's plot to deceive Isaac into passing the family blessing on to Jacob rather than Esau. (Genesis 27:23-27) Genesis 27:28-29 records the blessing that was conferred that day. After the deception was uncovered and the decision was made that Jacob would need to leave in order to escape the wrath of his brother, Isaac called his conniving son to him and blessed him another time. (Genesis 28:1-4) Although he had heard the covenant promises pronounced over him by the father on two different occasions, it would be totally anticipated that Jacob could wonder if these pledges could really be his considering how he had taken them through fraud. It was at that point that God Himself appeared to the wayward young man and reiterated the blessing. (Genesis 28:13-15) Again, the Lord spoke directly to Jacob that He would be with him as he returned to his father's land. (Genesis 31:3) After all these blessings from the patriarch of God and the very mouth of God Himself, why did Jacob feel that he needed a blessing from the angel? The answer seems simple – he had no faith and needed a miraculous sign for confirmation. Even though he got his miraculous sign (Genesis 32:27-30) and he was favorably received by his brother (Genesis 33:1-16), the fact that he hobbled the rest of his life as a reminder of the encounter makes me question whether we should actually credit him with having won the confrontation. Yes, he had a face-to-face encounter with

God, but it was an unnecessarily painful one and one that left a permanent disfigurement. How different was Jacob's limp when compared with the glorious illumination on the face of Moses (Exodus 34:29-35) who also had a face-to-face encounter with the Almighty (Exodus 33:11).

In order to truly comprehend God's perspective on who won that wresting match, we must turn to the book of Hosea.

> The Lord hath also a controversy with Judah, and will punish Jacob according to his ways; according to his doings will he recompense him. He took his brother by the heel in the womb, and by his strength he had power with God: Yea, he had power over the angel, and prevailed: he wept, and made supplication unto him: he found him in Bethel, and there he spake with us. (Hosea 12:2-4)

Here it is plainly said that Jacob prevailed – apparently a declaration of his victory. But notice that the proclamation of his triumph is in context of God's apparent displeasure in that He is described as having a controversy and being in the position to punish and recompense the actions and attitude of Jacob. Additionally, the prophet adds a statement about Jacob's weeping and making supplication – facts that are not recorded for us in the Genesis passage. We have no real context in which to interpret this statement, and even a cursory review of the academic studies that have been done by Jewish and Christian scholars alike will reveal that no one has a conclusive suggestion as to what Hosea was trying to say; however, I'd like to suggest the possible interpretation that Jacob eventually came to the place of regretting this bout with the angel. We should also notice that Hosea identifies the means by which Jacob prevailed against the angel –

his strength. Of course, we know that the Bible repeatedly decries our attempts to trust in our own strength or ability. (Psalm 20:7, 44:6, 49:6, 52:7, 146:3; Proverbs 3:5-6; Isaiah 31:1; Zechariah 4:6) In addition to the fact that Jacob likely came to realize that he had surrendered his faith in favor of his physique, it is likely that he also lamented that the one thing that he boasted in (his brawn) was forever disqualified because of the malady he suffered at the hand of that angel.

Why did Jacob think that he had to fight for a blessing when God had repeatedly blessed him at His own imitative? The answer is in the blessing that the angel spoke over him at the end of the struggle, "Thy name shall be called no more Jacob, but Israel: for as a prince hast thou power with God and with men, and hast prevailed." (Genesis 32:28) The bottom line was an identity crisis – he saw himself as Jacob (the supplanter – a scheming and conniving thief) – even up to the last second of the struggle. (Genesis 32:27) God, on the other hand, saw him as Israel (the prince with God). Jacob had already been positioned as prince since first blessing was that men (and specifically his brother Esau) would bow down to him. (Genesis 27:29, 29:40) Jacob's need was to be made aware of the fact that the power of God was already working inside him. (Ephesians 1:19, 3:7, 3:20)

The bottom line of this story seems to be that Jacob's real opponent that night was not an angel, but his own stubborn will and lack of faith in the promises of God and the God of those promises. He prevailed in that he didn't give up his struggle until he got an answer – much like the struggle I had in that parked car.

If this is the case, then Paul's request that the Roman believers strive together with him in their prayers to God (Romans 15:30) was likely a petition that they struggle in prayer to overcome their own doubts and desires for self-achievement. After all, these are the same people that the apostle had to admonish that they not be conformed to the mentality of the world but be transformed to the very mindset of God Himself. (Romans 12:2) These are also the ones whom Paul reminded that God would soon bruise Satan under their feet (Romans 16:20) – a promise that did not require their strength or struggle, just confident trust that God Himself would win the battle.

Of course, when we read Paul's prayer request in its full context we see that there was a definite intercessory element to the petition. He was asking that they pray for him – not themselves.

> Now I beseech you, brethren, for the Lord Jesus Christ's sake, and for the love of the Spirit, that ye strive together with me in your prayers to God for me; That I may be delivered from them that do not believe in Judaea; and that my service which I have for Jerusalem may be accepted of the saints; That I may come unto you with joy by the will of God, and may with you be refreshed. (Romans 15:30-32)

In that case, why would I even suggest that the striving in prayer has anything to do with the need for the Romans to overcome obstacles in their own faith? It is very likely that he wrote this letter during the winter that he spent in southern Greece during his last missionary journey as a free man. (Acts 20:2-3, I Corinthians 16:5-8) Therefore, his request that they pray for him on his journey to Jerusalem and onward to Rome (even though it turned out that he would be arriving there as a prisoner) is of immediate importance. Paul was a man who was unquestionably convinced within himself (Romans 4:21, 8:38; II Timothy 1:12), but he also knew that he was to meet many obstacles on the upcoming journey – not from the devil trying to stop him but from well-intentioned but misdirected believers who would try to dissuade him from his divinely appointed destiny. At this point, he needed intercession for the all-important agreement and backing of the Body of Christ. The story of the events that led up to his arrest in Jerusalem illustrates this principle. (Acts 20:17-21:15) Knowing that this would be his last opportunity to visit with the congregation of Ephesus in whom he had invested so much, he requested that the elders of the church meet him in Miletus when he made a stop there. He initiated the conversation he had with them with the statement that the Holy Spirit had testified repeatedly as he had traveled from city to city that bonds and afflictions awaited him upon his entry into the city of Jerusalem. He then added that he was not at all moved or disturbed by these foreboding messages because he was convinced within himself that he had served the Lord faithfully to that point and would complete his destiny with flying colors. His next port of call was Tyre where the believers tried to convince him not to continue his journey to Jerusalem because of the dangers that lurked there. Again, the apostle was unmoved by the emotional pleading of the saints and sailed on to Caesarea where there was an even more dramatic display of emotion as the prophet Agabus gave an illustrated message by tying him up in a belt and warning him that not only real fetters but also certain death awaited him in the Holy City. With emotional outcries and tears, the church members tried their best to convince Paul to him to alter his course, but Paul begged them to not break his heart with their pleadings. If these stories reflect the heart of the apostle and the general condition of the hearts of the believers with whom he was associated, then it is easy to see why he would write to them that they strive with him in prayer for him to be able to make it to Jerusalem and then onward to them in Rome.

The Christians in general were lacking in the faith it would take for him (and eventually the entire Body of Christ) to face the impending persecution and martyrdom. In essence, the striving that these believers were asked to do was ultimately more for their own good than for Paul's immediate need. Paul's struggle was not with the demonic spirits, but with supposedly Holy Spirit-directed fellow believers. The truth of the matter is that the devil wasn't trying to stop Paul from going to Rome because he thought that it would be the apostle's undoing through jail, torture, and his eventual execution.

Perhaps the story of Esther and her calling for a three-day fast can give us yet another window into the idea of striving in prayer. When word of the impending genocide of her people first reached Esther, she was unwilling to get involved. (Esther 4:7-11) However, Mordecai insisted that she search her soul over the matter and consider the fact that her Jewishness would eventually be discovered, dooming her to the sword just like all her other kinsmen. He then added that she consider that her unlikely rise to the position as the king's favored harem member was obviously no accident, but a strategic move on the part of God. (Esther 4:13-14) At which point, her answer came back that she was willing to put her life on the line to intervene for the Jewish people. Her only request was that the people accompany her in a fast. (Esther 4:16) But there is something significant in her request – she did not ask that the people intercede that the king would be receptive to her petition; she did not ask that they pray that the political tides be turned; she did not ask that they plead with God for their deliverance. No, her appeal was that the people's supplication be for herself personally. Apparently, she knew that there was still something inside her soul that needed to be dealt with – perhaps the fear of death that she was struggling with, perhaps her feeling of importance as a member of the royal household, perhaps guilt over having initially separated herself from her people and heritage, perhaps a feeling of inadequacy to state the issue in a compelling enough way to sway the monarch's heart. We have no way of knowing for sure, but it seems apparent that she somehow knew that her external mission could never be a success if she did not first successfully deal with her internal issues. Whatever her concern might have been, she knew that fasting was the proper approach for dealing with it. Even though she didn't use the words of Isaiah, it is likely that she conveyed his definition of fasting as she entered the three days of abstinence – afflicting of the soul.

> Is it such a fast that I have chosen? a day for a man to afflict his soul? is it to bow down his head as a bulrush, and to spread sackcloth and ashes under him? wilt thou call this a fast, and an acceptable day to the Lord? (Isaiah 58:5)

This passage comes from Isaiah's discourse on fasting in which he declares that the people had abused the practice of fasting. He then goes to great lengths to explain what should really be involved in a true fast. He says that a godly fast involves a change of heart by denying its self-centeredness and greedy nature. In other words, fasting is not actually a suppressing of the physical appetite but the mental process that makes us think that we must eat. Esther understood that the practice of fasting was actually a spiritual weapon that would help her pull down the strongholds and vain imaginations that were part of her soulical makeup. She knew that through fasting she would be able to control her thoughts, impulses, and urges – and take them captive, making them obedient! Then – having won the internal war – she was ready for the external battle.

A similar example can be seen in the life of David. When he and his fighting men returned to their home base at Ziklag to discover that their camp had been destroyed, their possessions plundered, and their wives and children had been taken hostage, his troops began to mutiny and threatened to stone him. (I Samuel 30:1-6) David's response was that he encouraged himself in the Lord. You see, he realized the all-important truth that real battle was won inside himself, not with his men or his enemy. Once he overcame the internal turmoil, he was ready to convince his army to refocus to pursue and defeat the enemy. When he heard God say to recover all, it was as good as done. (I Samuel 30:8)

The same principle can and will work in our lives as well!

The Prayer of Importunity

At this point, I think that it would be good for us to turn our attention to a couple of Jesus' sayings that have a lot to do with the way many people understand prayer – the story of the man who needed to borrow bread from his neighbor and the story of the widow and the unjust judge.

Let's begin with the story of the unfortunate man who received an unexpected guest on the same day that he had run out of bread.

> And he said unto them, Which of you shall have a friend, and shall go unto him at midnight, and say unto him, Friend, lend me three loaves; For a friend of mine in his journey is come to me, and I have nothing to set before him? And he from within shall answer and say, Trouble me not: the door is now shut, and my children are with me in bed; I cannot rise and give thee. I say unto you, Though he will not rise and give him, because he is his friend, yet because of his importunity he will rise and give him as many as he needeth. And I say unto you, Ask, and it shall be given you; seek, and ye shall find; knock, and it shall be opened unto you. For every one that asketh receiveth; and he that seeketh findeth; and to him that knocketh it shall be opened. If a son shall ask bread of any of you that is a father, will he give him a stone? or if he ask a fish, will he for a fish give him a serpent? Or if he shall ask an egg, will

he offer him a scorpion? If ye then, being evil, know how to give good gifts unto your children: how much more shall your heavenly Father give the Holy Spirit to them that ask him? (Luke 11:5-13)

This passage has often been used to present the message that we must tarry, labor, and travail in prayer until we get the desired results. In fact, I even know of a ministry that named itself after this passage because their major focus is to deliberately motivate lengthy and intensive prayer. Interestingly enough, the actual meaning is totally the opposite.

One of the first things that we have to realize about this story is that it is actually constructed with the intent of drawing a contrast rather than a comparison.

Notice that the gentleman who didn't want to give his neighbor the needed bread was called a "friend." Certainly, there is nothing wrong with seeing God as a friend. Moses was considered to be a friend of God (James 2:23), and Jesus told His disciples that He viewed them as His friends (John 15:15). However, we must realize that this terminology was used in the context of contrasting friendship with servanthood.

The Old Testament reference to the friendship of Moses and God states that Moses was able to speak face-to-face with God as two friends would converse. (Exodus 33:11) The cultural context of this statement would be the humble approach that a servant would make when entering the presence of his master – bowing low, possibly even prostrating himself on the floor, and definitely never making eye contact. In Psalm 123:2, David made the point that the servants' attention was on the hands of their masters rather than their faces, "Behold, as the eyes of servants look unto the hand of their masters, and as the eyes of a maiden unto the hand of her mistress." Remember that Esther – even as the queen – was not granted immediate access to her husband's presence. Esther 4:11 hints at the fact that she might not even have been permitted to make eye contact with her own husband in that she had to look for a signal of acceptance by his holding out his golden scepter – not an approving nod of his head. In contrast to this subservient relationship to a master where eye-contact is taboo, Psalm 32:8 depicts the relationship that God wants to have with us as one in which the instruction comes from carefully observing the facial expression and the glace of an eye – approval or disapproval by a nod or shake of the head; joy or suspicion by the widening or narrowing of the eyes; acceptance or questioning by deliberate eye contact or the rolling of the eyes; pleasure or dissatisfaction by a smile or a frown; a welcoming grin or a menacing scowl. In fact, God is so intent on having this kind of intimate communication with us that He directs us on at least seven occasions to seek His face. (I Chronicles 16:11; II Chronicles 7:14; Psalm 24:6, 27:8, 105:4; Proverbs 7:15; Hosea 5:16)

In the case of Jesus' declaring that His disciples are to be His friends, He specifically said that this relationship was an alternative to the servanthood role that they were anticipating. Even though friendship is a favorable relationship, it is far inferior to the relationship that Jesus is wanting to introduce to us. In the parable that we are studying, Jesus actually added an addendum that introduced a superior relationship – that of a father and a son that far surpasses the association between friends.

Jesus deliberately wove a number of significant details into the story that we must not overlook. The first fact that we should notice is that the gentleman was in bed. Since the Bible teaches us that God never slumbers or sleeps (Psalms 121:4), we should immediately recognize that the depiction is not intended to portray our God. However, it is in the response of the so-called friend that we should pay close attention to. Notice the number of times he referred to himself versus the singular reference to the petitioner, "Trouble <u>me</u> not: the door is now shut, and <u>my</u> children are with <u>me</u> in bed; I cannot rise and give <u>thee</u>." Additionally, we must note that the one reference to the man asking for bread is in a negative context – I can<u>not</u> rise and give thee." Such a response is totally out of character with what Jesus taught about the nature of God in the very next chapter, "Fear not, little flock; for it is your Father's good pleasure to give you the kingdom." (Luke 12:32) God is not self-centered, nor is He stingy. Therefore, we are in error when we use this story as an illustration to teach the need to struggle in persistent prayer to get an answer from Him. The final point that Jesus made about the supposed friend was that it was not his friendship – but the fact that he simply got fed up with his neighbor's persistence – that eventually prompted his "generosity." To apply such imagery to God is actually a sacrilege – if not a heresy!

  The follow-up comments from Jesus about asking, seeking, and knocking are also often misinterpreted by referencing the couple English translations that render the passage as "Keep on asking…keep on seeking…keep on knocking." (Amplified, International Standard Version) The implication that is then applied to the verse is that of persistence. However, the true meaning is not one of persistence but one of habitual asking, seeking, and knocking. In other words, Jesus was not teaching us to nag God over one request but to make a continual habit of feeling free to make one request after another. To illustrate the point, let's imagine that the scenario of an unexpected guest's midnight visit reoccurred. In such a case, do you think that the character in this story would even dare to impose on the reluctant "benefactor" a second time? My guess is that he would seek out another neighbor on this second predicament. Certainly, this is not what Jesus was trying to communicate. Quite the contrary – He wants us to realize that we can freely come to God with any request because He readily answers our requests.

Jesus concluded this discourse with the illustration of a father who gives his son exactly what he asks for – not a stone in place of a piece of bread or a serpent in place of a fish or a scorpion in place of an egg. He then intensified the illustration by stating that this was an evil father. How much more dramatic could He get – an evil father taking good care of his son? The obvious point that Jesus is trying to make is that if evil fathers give good gifts how much more reality God
– the good Heavenly Father – is going to give perfect gifts to His children! When Jesus used the wording "how much more" to speak of the Heavenly Father's eagerness to give spiritual blessings (Luke 11:13) along with all His physical gifts (Matthew 7:11) to His children, His intent was to help us to begin to see God in the light in which the Apostle Paul would later describe Him – the God who would do exceeding abundantly above all that we could ever imagine or dare to ask for. (Ephesians 3:20)

Let's now turn our attention to second story that most people interpret as a teaching about praying long and hard in order to get what we want from God.

> And he spake a parable unto them to this end, that men ought always to pray, and not to faint. Saying, There was in a city a judge, which feared not God, neither regarded man: And there was a widow in that city; and she came unto him, saying, Avenge me of mine adversary. And he would not for a while: but afterward he

said within himself, Though I fear not God, nor regard man; yet because this widow troubleth me, I will avenge her, lest by her continual coming she weary me. And the Lord said, Hear what the unjust judge saith. And shall not God avenge his own elect, which cry day and night unto him, though he bear long with them? I tell you that he will avenge them speedily. Nevertheless when the Son of man cometh, shall he find faith on the earth? (Luke 18:1-8)

Just think about the parable Jesus has presented to us. It is about a judge. Does Jesus teach us to relate to God as a judge? No, He teaches us that God is our Father. (Matthew 5:16, 45, 48 and 6:1, 4, 6, 8, 9 to list just a few places) He even tells us to go so far as to see Him as our Abba Father – our intimately loving "Daddy." (Mark 14:36) Does the scripture teach us that God insists that His children beg Him for the good things they need or want from Him? No, it teaches us that He will not withhold any good thing from those who love Him (Psalm 84:11) and that His eye is constantly going to and fro throughout the whole earth looking for an occasion to show Himself strong on behalf of His beloved. (II Chronicles 16:9) The scriptures even go so far as to say that He will give us more than we can even think or ask and that He answers even before we can ask! (Ephesians 3:20, Isaiah 65:24) If we know just this much about God, we can immediately realize that Jesus must not be teaching us to approach God like the widow approached the judge. With just a little contemplation, we will recognize that the unjust judge who did not fear God or have concern for men must be a contrasting image rather than a parallel picture of God. In other words, Jesus was using the story of the evil judge to paint a dark background against which He would portray the bright image of our Heavenly Father. The moral of the story is that if you can eventually get what you want from even the worst of people, how much more should we expect to receive answers from a God who is on our side. The truth is that He has even promised to answer <u>before</u> we ask – not after we beg and plead for it! (Isaiah 65:24)

Just think about it this way: if God was willing to give His only begotten Son for us when we were His enemies (Romans 5:10), do you think He is going to suddenly get stingy or make us beg for the simple little things we put on our prayer request lists? Instead, He proclaims that it is His good pleasure to give us His kingdom. (Luke 12:32)

The reference to God's answering prayers that are presented to Him day and night has given rise to a whole movement within the Body of Christ that advocates round-the-clock prayer chains, all-night prayer vigils, and twenty-four-hour prayer watches based on the concept that we need continual prayers that last all day and all night to get God's attention and response. However, the exact opposite is true. Jesus taught us not to pray long prayers full of repetition to try to get God to act for us. (Matthew 6:6-7) In contrast, when we have the kind of faith that is birthed out of a simple and genuine relationship with the Heavenly Father, Jesus promises that He will answer us speedily regardless of when we call on Him – whether day or night. Unlike the judge who sets the date for you to appear before him or even the doctor who tells his nighttime callers to take two aspirin and call him in the morning, our Lord is always ready to answer our prayers. Unlike Baal, our God is never caught napping. (I Kings 18:27) Instead of being drowsy or needing to be awakened, God was attentive to Elijah's request and answered his short sixty-three-word prayer with fire from heaven. (I Kings 18:36-37) Because Jesus understood that God was always attentive to His prayers, it took Him only a three-word prayer to bring Lazarus back from the dead. (John 11:42-43)

It seems to be such a simple passage when viewed from this new vantage point; however, we are met with one little hurdle to jump before we can be declared "home free" in this study. What did Jesus mean when He added the question, "Will the son of man find faith on the earth when he comes?" Two simple thoughts help us clear up that remaining question. The first is that we must understand this passage – as we must with all passages – by looking at it in context. The section just before this parable discusses the unexpected separation of folks at the end time. Jesus tells us that people who seem to be identical and who are doing exactly the same things will suddenly find themselves a quantum leap apart. Two will be working together; one will be taken and one will be left. Two will be walking together; one will be gone and one will stay. Two will even be together in the same bed (we don't get any more intimate than that); yet, even one of them will be left behind. The section after this parable is another parable about two men in the same place, doing the same thing. Again, they start out alike but end up lightyears apart. In this parable, Jesus helped us out a bit by giving us an explanation that serves not only for the story in which it was given but for this entire section of scripture. He said that the message was directed toward those who trusted in themselves. Indeed, one of the men in this latter parable demonstrated that he trusted in himself. He was certain that his fastings, prayers, and giving were his ticket into the kingdom of heaven. This thought actually leads us directly to the second thought that helps us understand the parable – what exactly

Jesus meant when He talks about faith. We all know the Hebrews 11:1 definition of faith; however, when asked what that definition means, we begin to stutter and stammer out some lame excuse or explanation, trying to cover up the fact that we really don't have a clue. However, a much better definition is found just ten verses later where the author of Hebrews said that Sarah counted Him who made the promise faithful to fulfill it. Sarah knew and lived by the conditions of true faith described in Hebrews 11:6, "But without faith it is impossible to please him: for he that cometh to God must believe that he is, and that he is a rewarder of them that diligently seek him."

    The problem that Jesus was confronting in His question was whether the Son of Man would find a church with true faith or if He would find a church full of people trusting in themselves who had accepted "faith substitutes." In Romans chapter four, the Apostle Paul drew our attention to another facet of the issue when he used Abraham's life to teach us about faith versus works. He illustrated for us that the patriarch was counted as righteous simply because he believed God. This was an act of faith that came without the law, ritual, or conformance to regulation; it was based purely on his relationship with the Lord. Anything – including our assumption that our lengthy persistent prayers can win us credit with God – that takes the place of a simple father-son relationship with God is a faith substitute. Just like many sugar substitutes, these alternatives should be labeled as hazardous to our health. We could learn a lesson from the commercial that tells us to accept no substitutes or from the soft drink that proudly proclaims itself as the real thing.

    Let me share a real-life story that humorously and tragically portrays how easy it is for us to become tricked into accepting substitutes for simple faith in God. One Saturday when I was still a college student, I joined a roomful of men for a prayer breakfast. One of their group came hobbling in because of an injury he had sustained at work on Tuesday of that week. Having suffered severely for four days, he was looking for a miracle during that prayer session. As was the custom in those days, he pulled a chair into the middle of the floor and sat down in the "hot seat" for prayer. Believing the biblical promise that he would recover when hands were laid on him (Mark 16:18), he anticipated a real miracle if he could get all fifty hands in the room laid on him. Before anyone had a chance to move toward the injured man, the leader of the group pulled him up from the chair. He explained that he had just returned from a Kathryn Kulhman meeting where he had seen so many miracles happen to those who had "fallen under the power." It was his advice that the brother stand during the prayer and anticipate his miracle to come if he fell to the floor. Before the gentleman had a chance to be slain in the Spirit, someone else who had been studying some of Kenneth Hagin's books began to instruct him that he had to believe and not doubt if he wanted to get what he said. Then a gentleman who had been listening to Kenneth Copeland's tapes began to interject something about the necessity of confessing the Word. I sat in the back of the room in utter amazement as the comments volleyed around the room from man to man as each one tried to tell the poor sufferer how to get healed. Suddenly, the room echoed with what sounded something like a Native American war whoop. We all looked around just in time to see the man who had asked for prayer leap so high into the air that his head almost touched the ceiling. He was shouting at the top of his lungs that God had sovereignly healed his back! There was no hot seat, no falling under the power, no name-it-

and-claim-it, no rebuking the devil – just the God who is eager to answer His children's requests!

Before we leave the topic of persistent prayer, we must take at least a few lines to address the story of Daniel's three-week-long fasting and prayer session. The story is recorded in Daniel chapter ten where we read that the prophet was given a vision of such import that it left him totally incapacitated and in a state of awe as he petitioned the Lord for twenty-one days for the explanation of the prophetic revelation. When the angel did eventually show up to answer the prophet's supplications, he had a very revealing message, "Fear not, Daniel: for from the first day that thou didst set thine heart to understand, and to chasten thyself before thy God, thy words were heard, and I am come for thy words. But the prince of the kingdom of Persia withstood me one and twenty days: but, lo, Michael, one of the chief princes, came to help me; and I remained there with the kings of Persia." (Daniel 10:12-13) Notice that the answer was dispatched as soon as the intercession began. The only problem was that there was a delay in the spiritual dimension. The messenger angel (whom many people assume to be Gabriel) was withstood by the prince of Persia (who is obviously a demonic force) until Michael (usually understood as the warrior angel) came to assist him. Many people read into this story the idea that believers need to travail in intercession to assist in the spiritual warfare in the heavens as they await the answers to their prayers. However, an unbiased reading of the passage doesn't have any indication that Daniel was actually involved in the warfare at all. He was simply waiting for the answer – which had actually been given the instant he made the request. The assistance that the messenger angel needed came from another heavenly being – not Daniel's human intercession. What a powerful revelation! Yet, this is only the tip of the iceberg in that this is still an Old Testament revelation. In that we now live in the New Testament experience, even this great eye-opener should be considered "old hat." Today, we live in the post resurrection reality where the devil is already a defeated foe without the ability to withstand the heavenly forces. (Colossians 2:15) Such a heavenly battle as described in Daniel's experience is simply a thing of the past for us; all we need is to realize what has already been done on our behalf. (Ephesians 1:17-22) The New Testament reality is that we now live in the day that Isaiah foresaw, "It shall come to pass, that before they call, I will answer; and while they are yet speaking, I will hear." (Isaiah 65:24)

Wrestling with Principalities

Okay, so maybe Esther's fast was not an all-out battle with the demon forces that were lurking behind Hamman's plot to destroy the Israelites and maybe Jesus didn't intend to tell us to practice importunity in pray when He told the stories of the widow and the man who needed to borrow bread, but we can't just discard the practice of fasting and prayer as a means of doing spiritual warfare against the devil. After all, we have the very words of Jesus Himself who told us that certain kinds of demons only come out through prayer and fasting. (Matthew 17:21, Mark 9:29) Let's take a look at the story behind our Lord's statement to see if we can grasp the full meaning of these words.

Jesus and His "inner circle" of Peter, James, and John had just been on the Mount of Transfiguration where Jesus miraculously manifested His divine glory and had a conversation with Moses and Elijah who had obviously been departed from this life for centuries. On the heels of this extravagant display of the supernatural, Jesus discovered that a crowd of spectators had gathered around the other nine disciples whom He had left at the foot of the mountain. Realizing that this was not a "flash mob" event, Jesus inquired as to why everyone was gathered and received the response that a gentleman had brought his son to the disciples to be delivered from demonic possession. Unfortunately, the disciples had failed to affect any change in the boy's condition. The description of the ensuing events paints quite a picture of the scale and intensity of the spiritual conflict that played out as Jesus confronted the powers of darkness that controlled the little boy. The demon took possession of the boy and threw him to the ground, where he lay wallowing in the dirt foaming at the mouth and gnashing his teeth. Then the poor victim fell into a motionless stupor. When Jesus rebuked the spirit, the lad shrieked out in anguish, began to convulse, and collapsed as if dead. The panic-stricken audience gasped upon witnessing what they assumed to be the poor boy's death right before their very eyes, but Jesus simply reached down and took the boy's hand and lifted him to his feet – totally restored and freed from the demonic attack. (Matthew 17:14-18, Mark 9:17-27)

When the disciples asked why they had not been able to set the boy free, Jesus responded that this kind comes out only through prayer and fasting – giving rise to a complete theology of fasting as a means of warring against demonic forces. At this point, I must stop long enough to interject that many reliable translations of the account in Mark do not include the word "fasting" in Jesus' reply. The omission is based on the fact that a number of the trustworthy ancient Greek texts only reference prayer rather than fasting and prayer as the key to getting results. It is entirely possible that the original version omitted the fasting element and that the versions that do include it were essentially borrowing from the wording of Jesus' response as it is recorded in Matthew's gospel. However, let's not engage ourselves in this particular argument at the moment and simply assume that Jesus did tell the disciples that they needed to practice both prayer and fasting. However, we must also re-examine the context of Jesus' answer to make sure that we really understand exactly what He was saying.

Thinking back to the discussion that Jesus had with the boy's dad, we remember that the father explained that the demon had often thrown his son into the fire and the water in attempts to take his life. Let's imagine what would have happened had Jesus responded that the demon could only be cast out after prayer and fasting and suggested a three-day fast like Esther called in the palace of Shushan. Such a notification of a set time would have given the demon a schedule to work with. It would likely be that when the father came back three days later, he would be looking to Jesus to perform a funeral rather than an exorcism.

Additionally, we have to notice how Jesus originally reacted when He was told of the disciples' failure, "O faithless generation, how long shall I be with you? how long shall I suffer you?" (Mark 9:19) Matthew's rendition of the story even adds the detail that Jesus called them "perverse," meaning "perverted, distorted, twisted, and corrupted." (Matthew 17:17) It sounds as if the people He was talking to – especially the disciples – were in essentially as bad a shape as the tormented lad! Furthermore, we must notice the father's response when Jesus told him that it would be possible for the boy to be set free if the father had faith. He tearfully cried out, "Lord, I believe. Help my unbelief." (Mark 9:24)

Now that we see the context of Jesus' explanation on why the disciples could not set him free, let's take a closer look at His actual response, "Because of your unbelief: for verily I say unto you, If ye have faith as a grain of mustard seed, ye shall say unto this mountain, Remove hence to yonder place; and it shall remove; and nothing shall be impossible unto you. Howbeit this kind goeth not out but by prayer and fasting." (Matthew 17:20-21) Notice that His answer centered around the unbelief that was inside the disciples – not on the demon that was inside the boy. A faithless generation, a father who fluctuated between believing and unbelief, and nine disciples who were handicapped by unbelief – it was the perfect formula for not being able to cast out the demon. Since Jesus' attention was on their unbelief, it seems only reasonable that His reference to "this kind" must have been intended to refer to this kind of unbelief rather than any specific kind of demon. In that case, we see the same pattern developing that we have seen in so many other scenarios – the real struggle is the internal one rather than the external one. If the disciples and the father could have conquered their unbelief – a struggle that involved prayer and fasting – then confronting and subduing the demon in the boy would have been no challenge.

However, there is a lot more to this story than we have looked at so far. In order to truly understand what happened at the foot of the Mount of Transfiguration, we have to back up several chapters to the story of Jesus' original commissioning of the disciples. In Matthew 10:1 and Mark 6:7, Jesus gave the disciples the power to heal the sick and cast out devils. Mark 6:13 and Luke 10:17 confirm that they actually were able to operate in that authority over demonic forces. Had the desperate father brought his son to them at this point, the story would have been totally different from the way we find it recorded a few chapters later. Why? Somewhere between this original commission and the episode at the foot of the Mount of Transfiguration, the disciples lost that authority by allowing themselves to be filled with unbelief. Jesus' remedy to such a malady is to practice a lifestyle of prayer and fasting to keep that of unbelief from invading and controlling their lives.

We don't know exactly how that unbelief got into their hearts. Perhaps it was at the news that John the Baptist had been beheaded. (Matthew 14:1-12, Mark 6:14-29) Interestingly, both accounts of the empowering of the disciples are followed immediately by the story of John's imprisonment. In Mark, the story of the beheading begins in the verse immediately after the statement that the disciples were actively casting out demons. In Matthew, the narrative of the beheading is separated by a long discourse, but the fact of John's arrest is immediately linked to the sending out of the disciples on their mission to heal, cast out devils, and preach the gospel. (Matthew 11:1-2) Even though we can't know for sure if this traumatic loss is what triggered their unbelief, we can see doubts and lack of faith beginning to manifest through the chapters between this event and the fateful day when they embarrassed themselves before a public audience. Peter made a faltering attempt to walk on water and sank after a few steps because of his lack of faith and his doubts. (Matthew 14:24-31) Peter's walking on water failed not because of the wind and the waves. After all, it's just as impossible to walk on calm water as it is to walk on stormy seas! His real problem was the fear inside himself. (Matthew 14:30) Jesus branded the entire company of disciples as faithless because they couldn't seem to grasp the significance of the multiplication of the fish and bread – even after they witnessed it on two separate occasions. (Matthew 16:5-12) Mark's gospel says that the disciples were suffering from hardened hearts at this point. (Mark 6:52, 8:17) Jesus went so far as to label Peter as Satan himself when he challenged the prophetic revelation of the coming crucifixion. (Matthew 16:21-23, Mark 8:31-33) As we walk with the disciples through these scenarios, we see the mounting struggle that culminated in the humiliating display of their loss of authority against the devil's emissaries – an outcome that could have been avoided by disciplining themselves through prayer and fasting. The bottom line is that if they had struggled with the work of Satan in their own lives, there would have been no conflict when they confronted with the devil in the little boy. Setting him free would have been "a piece of cake."

  The cartoon character Pogo once said, "We have met the enemy, and he is us." When we allow ourselves to forfeit our God-given position of authority, we actually become our own worst enemy. Paul acknowledged this problem and also offered a solution when he wrote to his young protégé Timothy, "In meekness instructing those that oppose themselves; if God peradventure will give them repentance to the acknowledging of the truth; And that they may recover themselves out of the snare of the devil, who are taken captive by him at his will." (II Timothy 2:25-26)

I began my class on the armor of God by reading Ephesians 6:12 to the class, "For we wrestle not against flesh and blood, but we do wrestle against principalities, against powers, against the rulers of the darkness of this world, against spiritual wickedness in high places." Several "Amen"s and "Hallelujah"s echoed around the classroom; so, I said, "Okay, I'll do that again." As I repeated the reading, a few more students joined in with their praises; so, I explained that I would have to read the verse again. By this time, the students were catching on that I was baiting a trap for them, and they refrained from any further responses. Thus, I insisted that I would read the verse yet again. Finally – on my fourth time to read the verse – one student interrupted, "But, Dr. Shirley, you're not reading the verse correctly." I then asked him to explain to the class what my error was, and he answered, "The verse doesn't say that we wrestle against the principalities, powers, rulers of darkness, and spiritual wickedness." With a great sigh of relief, I explained that this was the exact point that was I was trying to get them to see. Even though we almost always hear this verse preached with this meaning, the text does not actually say that we are ever to enter into combat with these demonic forces. At that point, I read the surrounding verses and pointed out that in verse eleven we are admonished to stand and that in verse thirteen we are told to stand and in verse fourteen we are commanded to stand. I then asked – that since the apostle instructed us to stand in three out of four verses –

what seems to be the logical imperative to insert for the missing verb in the one remaining verse. To my pleasure, the class seemed to catch on that the answer should be "stand" rather than "wrestle." Paul's prayer in Ephesians 1:18 that the eyes of their understanding would be enlightened was finally being answered!

The reason that these students were wary that I might have been luring them into a trap was that I had done exactly that same thing the day before when I waxed eloquent in preaching from Paul's words, "Having done all to stand, stand therefore." (Ephesians 6:13-14) After getting everyone – as the expression goes – into the "palm of my hand," I "lowered the boom" by telling them that all their enthusiastic backing and applause for my impassioned sermon were in total error. I then asked for a student from Nigeria to read the passage, adding in the punctuation. The reason that I wanted an African to read the verses is because they call a period "a full stop," helping make the point (pun intended) of the sentence more distinct: "Wherefore take unto you the whole armour of God, that ye may be able to withstand in the evil day (comma) and having done all (comma) to stand (full stop) Stand therefore (comma) having your loins girt about with truth…"

The problem with most interpretations of this passage of scripture is that we neglect the punctuation. When we leave out the commas and ignore the fact that the sentence ends before the "stand therefore" – which is actually the introductory phase to an entirely different thought – we get a totally different meaning from what Paul intended when he penned the verses. We interpret it as, "Having done everything we know how to do and when we have run out of all the tricks in our bag – then, when there is nothing else to do, we just staunchly keep on keeping on." That may be a good philosophy, but that is not what the scripture is saying. This scripture is telling us to put on the armor of God so we can do two things: withstand and stand.

Notice that there are a couple commas in this sentence. One comes after the word "day" and the other comes between the words "all" and "to." The commas indicate to us that there is a parenthetical phrase that has been added into the sentence. Adding a parenthetical phrase gives a little clarification to the whole sentence; however, this clarification is not necessary for the sentence to convey its intended meaning. We can remove the parenthetical phrase, and the sentence has exactly the same meaning. For example: in the sentence, "The teacher, not the students, is in charge of the class," the phrase "not the students" is a parenthetical phrase that is added in. It certainly clarifies the thought, but it is not necessary for the sentence to have meaning.

Taking the parenthetical phrase out of this verse gives us the basic meaning of the text. Without the added information, the sentence becomes easier to read, and we can see exactly what Paul is saying to us. The verse would then say, "Therefore, take up the whole armor of God that you may be able to withstand in the evil day…and to stand." This is the basic meaning of what Paul is saying here. The next sentence (which we usually blend into this thought) is actually a separate thought, separated by the "full stop." With this understanding, it is clear that Paul is telling us to take up the whole armor of God for two purposes: that in the evil day we can withstand and we can stand.

The parenthetical phrase that we dropped out of verse thirteen reads, "having done all." Some translations include the alternate wording "having overcome all" leaving the impression that we will be able to stand after we have defeated all our obstacles. Such a reading can be misleading in that it implies that we are the ones doing the overcoming when, in fact, it was Jesus Christ who won the victory through His crucifixion and resurrection. It seems more in keeping with the overall theme of the passage to keep the traditional reading, "having done all." Once we have touched all the bases that Paul has defined in the first five and a half chapters of the epistle, we finally come to the point of putting on our armor and taking our victorious stance. I am convinced that Paul was telling us that these foundational steps that he has enumerated up to this point must be completed before we can be assured of standing. The picture Paul is going to paint concerning spiritual warfare is far beyond what most Christians ever imagine or experience. The reason they drag from Sunday to Sunday and are always defeated, not knowing who is going to win – them or the devil – is that they have failed in implementing these foundational points. Pardon the advertisement, but I suggest that you get my book <u>Finally, My Brethren</u> for a full explanation of all the foundational truths that lead up to this point.

    Next, I asked for one of the students who had been a member of his high school's wrestling team to join me in front of the class. I needed him to describe the uniform that he wore as a wrestler. He mentioned that he wore a singlet, a small cap that covered his ears, and his athletic shoes. I then asked if he had ever seen pictures depicting wrestlers from the time of the New Testament. When he answered that he had, I asked him to describe the difference between his uniform and the ones that he had seen in the drawings. His response was that the Greek and Roman athletes didn't have any clothing at all. At the time of Paul's writing, these sports events occurred in the nude because they didn't want any hindrance in their movements. In fact, the Greek word for "gymnasium" literally means, "naked training." The idea of the nude wrestler is very appropriate when thinking of a confrontation with the devil. In Colossians 2:15, Paul described the devil as being naked, "And having spoiled principalities and powers, he made a shew of them openly, triumphing over them in it." The literal meaning of "spoiled" is "stripped him naked." The verse is actually rendered this way in some modern translations, vividly reiterating the scene being set here. The imagery behind this wording comes from the ancient practice of defrocking the kings and other political and military leaders of conquered nations. When those defeated enemies were brought back from the battle, they were totally humiliated by being marched through the streets naked – no longer with royal robes or regalia of rank. Through the wording here, Paul painted a vivid picture to awaken his reader to the fact that the opponent against whom we are to stand is an already defeated foe.

However, in order to confront this naked opponent, Paul tells us to put on the armor of God. Just imagine these principalities and wicked spiritual creatures in high places gathered together in their corner of the ring ready to have a wrestling match with the Christian, expecting him to come into the ring in his "birthday suit." The door opens from the other changing room and out comes the Christian dressed in a girdle, a breastplate, a helmet, shoes, a sword, and a shield. When the demons see a fully armored warrior walking out, you can imagine how they have to regroup. Just guess who will win such a wrestling match.

Next, I asked my wrestler to tell me exactly how much time he and his opponents spent in a standing position once the whistle blew to initiate the match. His answer was that the two opponents started in a locked position, but as soon as the referee gave the signal they were almost instantly on the mat. The match was spent tumbling and tossing on the floor until one was able to pin the other down and hold his shoulders to the mat for the ten count. Wrestling matches are not held standing up. But Paul told us time and again that our position is not tumbling nip and tuck on the floor. In this section of scripture, Paul is trying to tell us that our position is to stand. We are repeatedly told to put on the armor of God so that we will be able to stand. Our position is not a struggling position of wrestling and tumbling on the floor, but it is a victorious position of standing.

    Several years ago, I went to see the prehistoric pagan shrine Stonehenge in England on June 21, the only day of the year that the British government grants permission for people to go inside the fence surrounding the monoliths. The sun-worship cults demanded their religious rights and convinced the government to open the gates on this one day so they could do their ceremonies on this particular day when the sun rises over the central altar. As I was touring the site, one of the sun worshipers stood up and began threatening our group because he felt that we were desecrating the sun worshiper's event by talking. One of the guys in our group – a huge hunk of a man – walked around to the man making all the threats and started cracking his knuckles as if he were ready for a fight. The sun worshiper whimpered and went back to his devilish chants trying to pretend that we weren't there. Our "hero" did not have to get down and tumble on the ground. In fact, he never even had to do anything physical at all; he just walked toward our opponent and stood there. His massive presence demonstrated that he was in authority. When he cracked his knuckles, he sent out such a strong message that the challenger simply left us alone. The sun worshiper knew that he had met more than his match.

There, on the Salisbury Plain, I realized what Paul wanted us to know about what position we are to take in spiritual conflict – one of standing in authority, not one of wrestling in a desperate attempt to survive!

More Than Conquerors

Okay, so if Paul didn't intend for us to wrestle with principalities, why did he even introduce the topic of wrestling? In order to answer this question, I need to tell you about another of my little tricks that I sometimes play on my audiences. I will ask them how many of them are called to be pastors. After acknowledging them, I'll ask for those who are called to be evangelists. Once I have recognized them, I'll ask for the missionaries and so on. After I've been through all the ministry functions I can think of, I'll spring the trap by announcing that they are all wrong. Then I will read the first four verses of Ephesians chapter four, "I therefore, the prisoner of the Lord, beseech you that ye walk worthy of the vocation wherewith ye are called, With all lowliness and meekness, with longsuffering, forbearing one another in love; Endeavoring to keep the unity of the Spirit in the bond of peace. There is one body, and one Spirit, even as ye are called in one hope of your calling," stressing the words "one" and "calling." Next, I will explain that we all have one calling – not multiple callings – and that this calling is to build unity in the Body of Christ. I then comfort them a bit by continuing to read verses eleven through sixteen and reassuring them that Paul does validate all these special roles of leadership that they had labeled as their callings. However, I stress that the reason they serve in these roles is not for the sake of the positions themselves but for the purpose of building the Body of Christ to the point that it becomes one solidified unity that works together in harmony, manifesting the maturity of Christ Himself.

I then explain that the Roman army had shields that hooked together so that the soldiers did not go into battle as a number of individual warriors but as one massive advancing wall – providing maximum protection for each soldier. To illustrate the point, I draft a "volunteer" from the audience. I always ask for someone with a military background, preferably a decorated veteran who saw active combat during his deployment. As I hand him a shield, I keep him a bit distracted as I explain that the sword that I am holding was a gift from a Tuareg warrior from the Sahara Desert. Before he realizes what I'm doing, I suddenly thrust my sword around his shield and "score a hit." Of course, I always keep the sword in its sheath to avoid any possible injury to my unsuspecting victim. Next, I look for two additional "volunteers" – a skinny little girl who wouldn't weight more than ninety-eight pounds soaking wet and a frail old grandmother who would need help getting up to the stage. After placing the two ladies on either side of our now wounded warrior, I hand each of them a shield and show them how to connect their shields together. Once the three- member wall is in place it is easy to demonstrate that it is impossible to score a hit on the center target simply because he now has protection on each side. The significance of this illustration is that the two women who were now the warrior's bodyguards were definitely not the top military picks but they were his defense simply because they had come into unity with him. The translation into spiritual application is obvious. This is why Paul defines the shield of faith as being above all – literally, in front of everything else. (Ephesians 6:16)

But I'm not done with my illustration yet. Next I pull a random "volunteer" from the audience and stick a one-dollar bill in his pocket. Referencing Paul's admonition in Ephesians 4:28 that those who had been thieves must stop the practice of stealing, I reach over and pick my victim's pocket. After the audience sees his reaction to the crime, I ask him how he is going to respond to me in the future now that he knows that I am a pickpocket. Of course, his reply is that he is going to keep a safe distance so that I can't get to his pockets. Next, I follow up with the rest of Paul's instruction in the verse – that the ex-thief should get a job and earn a legitimate income so that he will have resources to bless those in need. I then slip the dollar bill back into the volunteer's pocket and ask him how he is now going to relate to me since he knows that I am now a giver rather than a taker. Of course, his response is that he is going to try to always be close enough to me so that I can reach his pocket in case the spirit of generosity happens to possess me again. The object of the lesson is that we separate ourselves when we do injurious things to one another but that we are drawn close together when we express love to one another. Applying this to the shield illustration, it is obvious that we can only link our shields when we are close together – a position that necessitates developing spiritual unity rather than carnal division. Picking up my sword again, I make the point that an attacker is always looking for a weak link so that he can get into the crack between the shields. Therefore, the real place to fight the battle is not against the attacker himself but against the internal conflicts within ourselves that make us want to separate from one another and delink our shields. This is why Paul tells us in the exact context of the reformation of the thief that we are to give no place to the devil. (Ephesians 4:27) When we stop wrestling with our brothers and sisters in the Body of Christ, we eliminate the place where the devil could potentially attack with the result that we have the ability to stand in resistance to the devil rather than the necessity to actually fight against him.

    Before I leave the topic of the interlinking shields that are part of the armor of God, I also point out that the apostle strategically picked his wording when he introduced the topic of the armor of God – "my brethren" – not "my brother" or "my brothers." His point is that we are not to see ourselves as an individual soldier (a brother) or even as individuals within a mob of soldiers (one of the brothers). We must be in unity as an army (the brethren) if we are to stand against the wiles, tricks, and schemes of the enemy.

Yet, there is one more significant point we must recognize – the fact that the apostle spends an extensive section of the Ephesian letter discussing family and business relationships as a lead-in to the topic of putting on the armor of God. (Ephesians 5:21-6:9) At first glance, this section may seem out of place, however, with the understanding that Paul is stressing the necessity of unity in the Body in order to stand against the enemy, it becomes clear that the text is actually very strategically positioned. The apostle is taking the message of unity out of the macrocosm of the church where we spend only a couple hours together each week and bringing it to the microcosm of the home where we live together twenty-four hours a day and the workplace where we rub shoulders forty hours every week. In essence, Paul is telling us that we have to get beyond theoretically acknowledging unity to the point of making it happen where "the rubber meets the road."

In Ephesians 4:3, Paul defined that keeping the unity of the Spirit in the bond of peace as "endeavoring" – meaning that it is striving that requires hard work. Later in that same context, he says that we are not to give place to the devil. (Ephesians 4:27) When we see the connection between these two statements, we can see that the struggle we have is not so much against the devil himself but against all the differences and contentions that would separate us from others in the Body of Christ. Yes, there is hard work and struggling involved; however, we overcome the hurdles and barriers that separate us, we eliminate the place the devil would otherwise get in. Thus, we eliminate having a face-to-face struggle with him!

The Old Testament is filled with war stories of intrigue, skirmishes, and bloody battles; however, there is one particular story that foreshadows New Testament realities -- the story of Jehoshaphat's face-off with the unified forces of Moab, Ammon, and Mount Seir. Jehoshaphat's immediate response was the same as Queen Esther's – fear. (II Chronicles 20:3) However, his remedy was also the same as Queen Esther's – to call a fast. In the process of the national supplication before the Lord, the king deliberately recited the covenant promises that the Lord had given to his nation and questioned God if He would not uphold them. (II Chronicles 20:6-12) The Lord's answer came back,

> Hearken ye, all Judah, and ye inhabitants of Jerusalem, and thou king Jehoshaphat, Thus saith the Lord unto you, Be not afraid nor dismayed by reason of this great multitude; for the battle is not yours, but God's. To morrow go ye down against them: behold, they come up by the cliff of Ziz; and ye shall find them at the end of the brook, before the wilderness of Jeruel. Ye shall not need to fight in this battle: set yourselves, stand ye still, and see the salvation of the Lord with you, O Judah and Jerusalem: fear not, nor be dismayed; to morrow go out against them: for the Lord will be with you. (II Chronicles 20:15-17)

Notice the similarities between this prophetic word and the message that we have seen in the epistle to the Ephesians: don't be afraid, set (position in unity) yourselves, and stand. They were not going to have to fight since the battle was actually the Lord's! The next morning, Jehoshaphat led his forces to the battlefield but employed one unusual strategy as he approached the battlefield – he positioned his singers ahead of his fighting men. (II Chronicles 20:21-22) The result was that the enemy forces were so confused that they wound up slaughtering one another, giving Israel the victory without having to "lift a finger."

To understand the logic behind this move, we have to remember that every army took with them singers that would essentially serve as the advance notification of their victories or defeats. When returning from battle, the singers would march ahead of the army – either singing a joyous song to announce their victory or a lament to denote their losses. Since these were the days before Facebook, the wives, mothers, daughters, and sisters of the fighting men had no way of knowing the fate of their husbands, sons, fathers, and brothers until they actually returned from the war. Therefore, they were always standing watch on the city wall awaiting that cloud of dust on the horizon that would herald the return of the army. Once they saw that distant dust, they would strain their ears to try to distinguish the tone of the melody that the musicians were singing. That way, they were able to brace themselves in advance for bad news or begin to rejoice for the celebratory return of their family members.

When the enemy forces witnessed the joyous singers leading the troops, they could only surmise that something had happened behind the scenes that had ensured the Israelites' victory. Their assumption was that one of their coalition forces had turned against them and sided with Jehoshaphat – prompting them to attack the supposed traitors among them. At the end of the day, the army of Israel was the unquestioned victor – even without fighting! Moreover, they walked away from the battlefield with a fortune in the spoils of war. (II Chronicles 20:25)

The Apostle Paul had a term that he used to describe this sort of situation – "more than conquerors." (Romans 8:37) The best way to explain this term is that a conqueror is someone who goes into battle, faces the enemy, gets bloody and bruised, but walks away victorious. The ones who are more than conquerors are his wife and family back home who enjoy the freedom and prosperity that the brave warrior purchased with his sacrificial courage. The bottom line is that those who are more than conquers enjoy all the benefits of the victory without having to enter into the conflict that secured them. In the spiritual dimension, Jesus is the conqueror in that He fought with the enemy and won (Genesis 3:15) and we are more than conquerors when we freely receive the benefits that He has secured for us (Romans 3:24, 8:32; I Corinthians 2:12).

Let's not abdicate our position as more than conquerors by trying to get into unwarranted battles in our own attempts to fight against the enemy – especially since he has already been defeated. (Colossians 2:15)

Kingdom Violence

Having determined that we are more than conquerors and that taking the aggressive position of a conqueror would actually be abdicating our higher position, we must give some attention the words of Jesus in which He seems to indicate that we should actively struggle against the devil in order to conquer him. Matthew 11:12-15, Jesus said, "And from the days of John the Baptist until now the kingdom of heaven suffereth violence, and the violent take it by force. For all the prophets and the law prophesied until John. And if ye will receive it, this is Elias, which was for to come. He that hath ears to hear, let him hear." Luke records this same discourse, "The law and the prophets were until John: since that time the kingdom of God is preached, and every man presseth into it. And it is easier for heaven and earth to pass, than one tittle of the law to fail." (verses 16:16-17) This statement has given birth to a whole movement of teaching concerning violently struggling against the forces of evil in order to take the kingdom of God away from the devil. However, in light of the fact that Jesus also taught us that it is God's good pleasure to give us the kingdom (Luke 12:32), we should rethink the whole idea of having to violently take something that has been readily given to us. After all, the New Testament repeatedly tells us that the just live by faith – not violence (Romans 1:17, Galatians 3:11, Hebrews 10:38) – and that mercy, grace, peace, and love – not aggression – are to be multiplied in our lives (I Peter 1:2, II Peter 1:2, Jude 1:2). Perhaps we have been reading something different into the passages from what our Lord actually intended.

One of the most important principles to remember in trying to interpret scripture is that we have to treat it like a piece of real estate. When determining the value of a piece of land, there are three important factors to take into account: location, location, location. The same is true with the scripture; we must evaluate the passage in its context. The passages immediately before and after these verses about the kingdom of God deal with living under the Old Testament law. When Jesus said that violent men would press into God's kingdom, He was telling the people that a transition was coming from the period of the law to the age of grace. The dispensation of the authority of the law and the prophets came up to the time of John the Baptist who was spoken of as the final prophet to come just before the appearance of the messiah. (Matthew 11:10) The Pharisees did everything they could to live by the law, and they reacted dramatically when they encountered anyone who did not join them in their diligence for the letter of the law. When John the Baptist came fasting, they accused him of having a demon because he didn't eat like them. But when Jesus ate with them and even turned water into wine, they called him a demoniac, a glutton, and a winebibber. (Matthew 11:18-19) They were happy with the *status quo* and wanted everything to stay the same under the authority of the Old Testament law. They had worked for fifteen hundred years to set up their legal traditions and "sacred cows." They had in place all their intricate interpretations that allowed them to get around the regulations of the law that they could not meet. They were content; but, all of a sudden, there appeared a man who came to introduce a new generation that would shake and even remove their world. They resisted because they didn't want to lose their place and their authority under the law.

Bias – the Greek word used in Luke sixteen for "violent" and translated as "take it by force" in Matthew – means "by compulsion." It was used in the Greek to speak of a conscientious objector who was compelled by his government into military service when he didn't want to fight and thought that it is morally wrong to do so. The term was also used for sexual compulsion when a person lost all moral control. *Bias* is also translated as "mighty" in Acts 2:2, "And suddenly there came a sound from heaven as of a rushing mighty wind, and it filled all the house where they were sitting." It was a wind of compulsion. The one hundred twenty believers in the Upper Room didn't make up the languages they were speaking or select the words they were saying. Instead, there was an outside force like an invisible ocean wave that swept over them and compelled them to say things that they otherwise would not be able to vocalize. In Matthew 12:24, we see how the Pharisees were pressing in on Jesus and accusing Him of taking away the kingdom of the law that they so preciously wanted to protect, "But when the Pharisees heard it, they said, This fellow doth not cast out devils, but by Beelzebub the prince of the devils." The violent legalists rose up to press against the kingdom of God as Jesus came to establish it. In Luke 11:17-21, we see Jesus' response,

> But he, knowing their thoughts, said unto them, Every kingdom divided against itself is brought to desolation; and a house divided against a house falleth. If Satan also be divided against himself, how shall his kingdom stand? because ye say that I cast out devils through Beelzebub. And if I by Beelzebub cast out devils, by whom do your sons cast them out? therefore shall they be your judges. But if I with the finger of God cast out devils, no doubt the kingdom of God is come upon you. When a strong man armed keepeth his palace, his goods are in peace.

When Jesus used the illustration of a strong man

protecting his goods when a stronger one came in, He – of course – was speaking of Himself and His followers as the stronger one. The stronger man overcame the strong man and took from him all his armor. The devil's armor is the authority (*exousia*) that he exerts through his lying and deceptive words. Because we are the ones with the greater one living inside of us (I John 4:4) and we are more than conquerors (Romans 8:37), we are the ones in position to rip off all the armor that the devil is trusting in by destroying those thoughts which try to raise themselves above the knowledge of God (II Corinthians 10:3-5). We rip off the devil's armor by speaking the truth. We bind the strong man by using the belt of truth, the gospel of peace, and the sword of the Spirit as weapons against the deceptive lies of the enemy. We can refute what he says by proclaiming the truth of the Word. That will bind up everything he says and his *exousia* will taken away. Because we have more strength and because the truth is stronger than his lies, we can take his possessions. The Greek word used here for "strong" and "stronger" is *iskuros* that means "having physical strength." Yes, the enemy has some physical strength; however, this passage says that we have more because we are stronger. When comparing our strength with that of the enemy, Paul said that our strength was actually exceedingly great in comparison to any strength that the devil has. (Ephesians 1:19) We are not just a tad stronger; we are immeasurably stronger than our enemy. When the devil flings his lies, we can speak words of truth and demonstrate the fact that we are stronger.

Mark 3:29-30 reminds us, "But he that shall blaspheme against the Holy Ghost hath never forgiveness, but is in danger of eternal damnation: Because they said, He hath an unclean spirit." When the Pharisees called the work of the Holy Spirit the work of an unclean spirit, it was blasphemy against the Holy Spirit. They were educated men who knew the law. They knew the scriptures of the coming of the messiah. They should have been able to recognize the power of God in their day of visitation. They were not unlearned or ignorant men who, without calculation, had thrown off Jesus; they were in danger of blaspheming the Holy Spirit because they knew what they were doing and determined to do it anyway. When people have that violent compulsion to come against the kingdom of God, they are getting close to blaspheming the Holy Spirit – an ultimately serious thing because it is unforgivable. At that point, we have to recognize that our ability to step in and bind the strong man and pull off his armor and plunder his house is the thing that will determine their eternal destiny – whether they can ever get forgiveness or whether they will face eternal damnation. We have to step in, bind the strong man, and set the captives free. If we don't, they are very close to stepping across the line into an unforgivable situation. It is a matter of life and death – not only for our own sakes, but also for the sake of those to whom we minister and even those who oppose us – that we know how to use our armor and our weapons. In essence, Jesus was not telling us that we need to be violent to get the kingdom; he was saying that those who would oppose us are the violent ones and that we must step in as the stronger ones and rescue them <u>into</u> the kingdom by destroying the enemy's lies and releasing them through the truth. (Colossians 1:13)

    Having mentioned our commission to bind the strong man and then release his captives through the truth, we must remember that Jesus actually defined our role of binding and loosing as the literal keys to His kingdom – an all-important point to consider in that we don't have to violently contend for entrance into a kingdom if we already have the keys that open its gates. In Matthew 16:19, Jesus said, "And I will give unto thee the keys of the kingdom of heaven: and whatsoever thou shalt bind on earth shall be bound in heaven: and whatsoever thou shalt loose on earth shall be loosed in heaven." This statement has given rise to a whole theology of binding and loosing as an approach to warfare against the devil, but – before we jump to any conclusions as to what He was intending to say here – let's take a minute to look at some more modern translations of this passage:

> I will give you the keys of the Kingdom of the Heavens; and whatever you bind on earth shall remain bound in Heaven, and whatever you loose on earth shall remain loosed in Heaven. (Weymouth's New Testament)
>
> And I will give the keys of the kingdom of Heaven to you. And whatever you may bind on earth shall occur, having been bound in Heaven, and whatever you may loose on earth shall occur, having been loosed in Heaven. (Modern King James Version)
>
> And I will give to thee the keys of the reign of the heavens, and whatever thou mayest bind upon the earth shall be having been bound in the heavens, and whatever thou mayest loose upon the earth shall be having been loosed in the heavens. (Young's Literal Translation)

Notice that the wording in each of these renditions of the passage suggests that what happens in heaven is not the result of what is done on earth; rather, it is actually a pre-existing condition. Weymouth's Translation uses the word "remain," implying that the determination is already made and that our use of the key to heaven's window is essentially a spoken affirmation in agreement with what is already predetermined. The Modern King James and Young's Literal Translation both use the wording "having been," which again reflect the idea that the outcome is already determined prior to the prayers or proclamations of believers. All these translations are making an attempt to convey the actual message of the Greek text, which implies that the key Jesus was giving us was not the ability to self-determine destinies and outcomes. Rather it is the ability to know the mind of God well enough that we are actually speaking out His mind on the matter whenever we pray or proclaim anything. (I Corinthians 2:16) To get a clear vision of what Jesus was trying to tell us, let's look at a very familiar – yet often misunderstood – passage on intercession:

> And take the helmet of salvation, and the sword of the Spirit, which is the word of God: Praying always with all prayer and supplication in the Spirit, and watching thereunto with all perseverance and supplication for all saints. (Ephesians 6:17-18)

As we have already seen, Paul is making an intentional connection between prayer and the Word of God in that he lists both of them as being connected with the Spirit. Remembering a few other biblical truths, we can begin to see the message behind this connection. According to Psalm 119:89, God's Word is forever settled in heaven. Even though His ways are much higher than our ways (Isaiah 55:9) and His judgments beyond finding out (Romans 11:33), He has made a way through the work of the Holy Spirit for us to know all the benefits He has prepared for us (I Corinthians 2:9-10, John 14:26). When the Holy Spirit reveals to us the specific promises from the Word of God that we need to use as the sword of the Spirit when He is directing our prayers, then we develop a confidence in our prayers (I John 5:14-15) and an assurance that everything is going to work out just right (Romans 8:26-28). In I Corinthians 14:15, Paul gave us a hint as to how all this can work in our prayer lives, "What is it then? I will pray with the spirit, and I will pray with the understanding also: I will sing with the spirit, and I will sing with the understanding also." I apply this principle to my prayer time by spending some time in prayer in the spirit, allowing the Holy Spirit to awaken in me some specific needs and also some specific promises related to these needs. Then I shift to prayer in the understanding, interceding that these biblical promises would be fulfilled in the lives of those for whom I am praying. God already has our success determined in heaven, but we need the ability to pray under the direction of the Holy Spirit so that our prayers are not off base – but in total alignment with what God has already bound and loosed in heaven. Certainly this is why Jesus made the prayer that God's will be done on earth as it is in heaven a major point in His model prayer. (Matthew 6:10, Luke 11:2)

    If we are praying incorrectly and do not know how to pray or what to pray for, then we will have ineffective prayer. Years ago, just before the dawn of the computer age, a student of mine told me that she had been praying for a very long time for a new typewriter. She had a certain kind in mind and asked very specifically for that kind of typewriter. After I counseled her concerning praying in the will of God, she asked the Lord to just give her whatever He wanted her to have. Within a couple days, she was given a computer that was an incredibly better typing system than even the best typewriter she had been wanting. She could have gotten a much quicker response had she known how to pray from the beginning. Generally, there are two ways to know that our prayers are in the perfect will of God rather than in our own human will: to pray according to the Bible (because the scripture is the express will of God) and to pray according to the Holy Spirit (because the Holy Spirit is the revealer of the express will of God). It is important to search the scriptures and know exactly what God's Word says about our specific request. Once we find a promise or a principle that speaks to our need, we should lock into that scriptural truth and use it as an anchor for our prayers. In addition, we should always pray in the Spirit over our needs. The Holy Spirit always prays in accordance with the will of the Father and, therefore, prays a perfect and effectual prayer. (Romans 8:26-28) Another type of knowledge needed for effective payer is the knowledge of the nature of God. Sometimes we may not know the exact will of God, but we could determine it by knowing what is in alignment with the personality and character of God. For instance, the lady who was praying for the typewriter had no way of knowing that God's will was to give her a computer rather than a typewriter. However, she finally decided to pray in accordance to the nature of God, which is that He is the giver of all good gifts. (James 1:17) Because she prayed in confidence that whatever He would give her would be the best thing that she could get, she received a gift that was far better than what she would have picked on her own!

Therefore, if there is any struggle suggested in Jesus' statement about binding and loosing, it is the struggle to get ourselves in alignment with the mind of God enough so that we can intelligently know what He has already bound or loosed in heaven so that we can effectively agree with Him and bind or loose those things in our own lives and in the lives of those for whom we pray.

Seeing these two principles together – the violent assault against the kingdom and using the keys of binding and loosing – we come to a clear understanding of what Jesus was trying to say. Every time the kingdom of God is preached, there will be a violent force that will rise up against the power of the gospel. The world will compulsively – beyond its own will – turn against us and the kingdom of God. The attack is not against us personally. It is against the gospel that we preach. Those who rise up against us are not working in their own will; they are being compelled to do so. Rather than taking offense personally, we must realize that our real enemy is the deception of the devil that is compelling those who oppose us. We can bind the strong man because we are stronger than the devil. We can loose the goods he has stolen – the very souls of the men through whom he has been perpetrating his violence. Of course, the key is that we have the mind of Christ so that we can understand what our role is to be. God has already bound the devil's angels (II Peter 2:4), but their influences are still active in the world. To understand this principle, we need only to think of the Apostle Paul, who was in a dungeon but was still able to write and distribute epistles that have changed the world (II Timothy 2:9); John Bunyan who penned <u>Pilgrim's Progress</u>, one of the greatest pieces of English literature ever written that has been translated into more than two hundred languages and never been out of print since 1678, while in Bedford Prison; Dietrich Bonhoeffer who impacted the world from a Nazi concentration camp; and Nelson Mandela, who pioneered a new Africa from inside the walls of his jail cell. In the same way that these great men of God were able to exert tremendous influence even while incarcerated, the demonic forces are still manipulating the hearts and minds of men. It is our place to bind up their influence by taking captive every vain imagination, every high thing that exalts itself against the knowledge of God, and every thought and bringing them into the obedience of Christ. (II Corinthians 10:5) We must also realize that Jesus has already loosed the captives (Luke 4:18, (I Timothy 2:4) but that they can't experience that liberty until we as believers share the gospel with them. Jesus told us that our job is to make disciples of all the nations (Matthew 28:19). He also taught us that discipleship in the key to receiving the knowledge that sets men free. (John 8:31-32) Therefore, it is our responsibility – through ministering the gospel –to loose on earth the men that He has already loosed in heaven. With this new insight into the passage, we can come to the understanding that we are not so much in a struggle with the powers of darkness to gain possession of the kingdom for ourselves; rather, we are called to exert the power and authority that we have been given in order to rescue those who are captive in the grips of the devil's compulsively violent kingdom of darkness.

The Armor of God

One important fact that we must not overlook is that Jehoshaphat sent his army to the battlefield in full combat attire even though he knew in advance that they would not lift a sword in the conflict that day. Likewise, Paul tells us to put on the whole armor of God even though he knows that the armor is for the purpose of standing in authority rather than struggling in conflict against the enemy. With that in mind, let's take fresh look at the elements of our armor and see if there may be some aspects of their significance that we could have possibly overlooked.

First, Paul mentions the girdle of truth – closely paralleling a belt or a harness. The function of this piece of equipment was to hold the weapons that the soldier would be carrying. At this point, I need to beg your patience since I am not ready to discuss these weapons; however, let me ask you to remember one significant fact when we do get to that topic – that the thing that supports these weapons is truth. A second function of the girdle was to serve to hold up the robe of the warrior when he wanted to shorten it from an ankle-length garment to knee-length attire to allow more mobility. Since we in the Western world are not accustomed to seeing men in skirts, the idea may be foreign to us; however, it is a common sight in places like Sri Lanka where men wear sarongs and Myanmar where they wear lungis. Both of these skirt-like garments can be tucked up at the waist in order to allow the men to run faster and move without restrictions. Spiritually, the only way to have real freedom is to live in truth, dispelling all lies. (John 8:31-32) One additional function of a girdle is that it can serve as a brace to support a worker as he does heavy lifting – helping him to avoid back injuries and hernias. If we are not armed with the truth, we are susceptible to the lies of the enemy and ultimately to his scheme to injure and ultimately destroy us. (John 8:44)

There are a number of areas of truth that are significant in establishing the strength, protection, and freedom that guarantee our victorious position when we have to stand against our enemy – and Paul explores each of them in the first five and a half chapters of Ephesians leading up to the discussion of the armor of God. One of the major areas is our relationship with ourselves. Notice the number of times that he made reference to the the heart – indicating the necessity to have an inner integrity in which our lives are in total unity with our outward man and our inner man in agreement. In Ephesians 4:18, he contrasts our lives with the lives of the unregenerate who have their understanding darkened and are alienated from the life of God through the ignorance in their inner being – the result of being blinded in their hearts. In Ephesians 6:5, the apostle admonishes us to live out our responsibilities in life in singleness of heart – without the hypocrisy of having one attitude in our hearts while portraying something contradictory on the outside. In the following verse, he clarifies the point even further by saying that this is actually a spiritual principle because the foundational reality is that in doing so we are manifesting the will of God from our hearts. (Ephesians 6:6) This introduces another all-important arena of truth – our relationship with God. In fact, Paul actually equates our interactions with God Himself to truth – the girdle that he wants us to equip ourselves with – in at least two different places in this epistle. (Ephesians 4:21, 5:9) Of course, we have already seen that the paragon of the Christian life is manifested in our relationship with others when he says that by becoming unified with one another, we actually manifest the image of Christ. (Ephesians 4:15, 4:25)

The second element that Paul presents is the breastplate of righteousness – a protection for the heart. When we do, think, or say something good and noble, the first reaction that we have is a warm sensation in our hearts. Likewise, when we think, do, or say something wrong, the first way that we realize our error is from a little prick in our hearts – what we call our conscience. Even though some have given the conscience a "bad rap" based on I John 3:20 "For if our heart condemn us, God is greater than our heart, and knoweth all things," John goes on in the following verse to validate the work of the conscience, "Beloved, if our heart condemn us not, then have we confidence toward God." In fact, the scriptures teach us that our consciences serve a significant role in preserving our godly status. (Acts 23:1, 24:16; Romans 9:1: II Corinthians 1:12, 4:2; I Timothy 1:5, 1:19, 3:9; II Timothy 1:3; Hebrews 9:14) That little voice within us that directs us toward righteousness is a vital element in protecting our hearts and guaranteeing a secure place for us in the Body of Christ. One of the most intriguing examples of the power of a Holy Spirit-inspired conscience comes from the life of Dr. Lester Sumrall. When he was ministering among a tribe in a very remote rainforest in South America, he led a number of women to salvation. Afterwards, they asked him if he might have a few pieces of extra cloth in his backpack. When he questioned them about their request, they replied that they would like something to cover their breasts. His response was one of curiosity – why they had this sudden concern for modesty in that they had nothing in their culture to even suggest that a woman's breast should not be exposed. Their reply was that they had no idea why they felt this way but that something inside them just told them that it would be a good idea. This is the power of a conscience that is born out of a relationship with God.

Such a conscience is a godly breastplate protecting us from error.

The next elements that the apostle presents are the shoes of the preparation of the gospel of peace. As we have already explored, the one calling that we all have is to keep the unity in the Spirit in the bond of peace. Additionally, Paul admonishes us to walk worth of that calling – a directive that requires that we have shoes adequate for the task. Just as we have different kinds of athletic shoes specialized for the different activities that we desire to excel in, we must have shoes that appropriately equip us for the task of unifying our brothers and sisters in peace. Interestingly, Paul tells exactly what those shoes look like – lowliness, meekness, longsuffering, and forbearing one another in love. (Ephesians 4:2)

Next comes the shield of faith – the interlocking shields that we have already seen as being of ultimate significance in our ability to stand against the devil.

The helmet of salvation refers to having our head protected by salvation. Paul challenged us in Romans 12:2 that we not be conformed to this world but be transformed by the renewing of our minds – thinking like saved people rather than like the natural people of the world. In Ephesians 4:17, he defined the mentality of the natural man as vanity – or emptiness. Of course, it is easy to immediately define vanity as "emptiness" and go on – totally missing what this verse really has to say. To really catch on to what Paul was trying to communicate, we need to review the book of Ecclesiastes where Solomon defined exactly what vanity entails – a study that we did in detail in the first volume in this trilogy, <u>Good People, Bad Things, and Vice Versa</u>. Solomon left us with essentially "no stone unturned." Every area of human interest and endeavor – business, industry, finance, education, politics, religion, entertainment, family – is included as being vanity. Thus, it becomes obvious that the Apostle Paul wasn't saying that natural humans don't have anything in their brains; rather, he was trying to tell us that the things that they occupy their minds with have no substance. Even if their plans and schemes move nations, transfer fortunes, and change the course of history, they are still vanity in God's sight. In that case, what is it that must be planted so that our minds as believers will not be focused on such vanity? Paul answered this question by sharing his own testimony in Philippians chapter three.

> Though I might also have confidence in the flesh. If any other man thinketh that he hath whereof he might trust in the flesh, I more: Circumcised the eighth day, of the stock of Israel, of the tribe of Benjamin, an Hebrew of the Hebrews; as touching the law, a Pharisee; Concerning zeal, persecuting the church; touching the righteousness which is in the law, blameless. But what things were gain to me, those I counted loss for Christ. Yea doubtless, and I count all things but loss for the excellency of the knowledge of Christ Jesus my Lord: for whom I have suffered the loss of all things, and do count them but dung, that I may win Christ. (verses 3:3-8)

In this passage, Paul gives us a pretty impressive list of accomplishments and pedigrees that would certainly qualify as the "stuff" of success in almost every dimension of life. Yet, he says that all these things are essentially dung – vanity, if you prefer a little more polite description. The one thing that he says is worthy of his consideration is "the excellency of the knowledge of Christ Jesus my Lord." The truth is that the New Testament abounds with confirmations of the fact that the knowledge of God is the essence of the Christian life. (Romans 1:28, 10:2, 11:33; I Corinthians 15:34; II Corinthians 2:14, 4:6, 10:5; Ephesians 1:17, 3:4, 4:13; Colossians 1:10, 3:10; II Peter 1:2, 1:3, 1:8, 2:20, 3:18)

It is the knowledge of our Lord and Savior Jesus Christ that must be planted in us to take the place of the vanity that will otherwise fill the thoughts of our minds and hearts. (Ephesians 3:17, Colossians 1:23, 2:7)

The final element to the armor of God that Paul mentions is the sword of the Spirit, which he defines as the Word of God. He goes on in the following verse to speak of praying in the Spirit in what seems to be a deliberate situating of two thoughts in parallel positions so that we realize that they are to be seen in relationship. Since the sword is the the sword of the Spirit and prayer is also the work of the Spirit, we can assume that Paul was wanting us to realize that our sword is activated through prayer. Additionally, he tells us that our sword is the Word of God – implying that our effective prayers are those that are prayed when we use the Word of God as inspired by the Spirit of God. (Romans 8:26-28, I John 5:14-15, James 5:16) This is the exact weapon that Jehoshaphat used in coming to the place that he could put his fears behind him and receive the prophetic assurance that he was more than a conqueror and could go into the confrontation with his enemy – knowing that God was doing the fighting and that he could simply stand on the sidelines and rejoice in the victory!

This brings us the question of why Christians do struggle with apparent attacks from the devil if our position is to simply stand and watch as the Lord defeats all our enemies for us. Let's call upon the Apostle Paul to share his own personal testimony at this point. When harassed by a tormenting spirit, he cried out to the Lord for deliverance and was answered that he did not need external divine intervention. In fact, the authority he needed to combat and overcome his demonic foe was already inside him.

> And lest I should be exalted above measure through the abundance of the revelations, there was given to me a thorn in the flesh, the messenger of Satan to buffet me, lest I should be exalted above measure. For this thing I besought the Lord thrice, that it might depart from me. And he said unto me, My grace is sufficient for thee: for my strength is made perfect in weakness. Most gladly therefore will I rather glory in my infirmities, that the power of Christ may rest upon me. (II Corinthians 12:7-9)

There has been a lot of confusion and controversy among those who would try to interpret the passage. When Paul spoke of his thorn in the flesh, many people get confused and fail to follow the logic that the real problem is demonic. The difficulties are based on several misconceptions which people hold in their minds when they read the scripture.

The first difficulty arises from the word "exalted." Many Bible scholars assume that the apostle is saying that there was a danger that he might get too proud because of the revelations he had received – that he would become, as a mother might say of a little boy who was getting a little too cocky for his age, "too big for his britches." They think that Paul was suggesting that he might fall prey to the same trap about which he warned the Corinthians in his first letter to them: being puffed up through knowledge. (I Corinthians 8:1) In answer to this question, we must remember that our Heavenly Father is the giver of all good and perfect gifts (James 1:17), that He is a perfectly wise God (Romans 16:27, I Timothy 1:17, Jude 1:25), and that the blessings He gives us add no sorrow with them (Proverbs 10:22). Therefore, the gift of the revelation that Paul had received was not something that could have endangered him. Quite the contrary – the devil knew that he was the one in danger of being hurt if Paul's revelation would be widespread. Therefore, he was doing everything within his power to keep Paul from being exalted to a platform from which he could preach this damaging message.

The second misconception centers on the source of Paul's thorn. Many scholars assume that it was God who put this thorn into Paul's life. However, we need to step back from the passage a bit and look at it in a broader scope to get a clear understanding. Consider the logic – or rather, lack of logic – in the assumption that God gave Paul this thorn. If God knew that the revelations He was giving Paul were possible sources for him to fall into error, certainly He would not correct the situation by inflicting some sort of difficulties. There is no biblical precedent for God's having put bad things in His people's lives as a preventative. God's pattern for preventing His people from going astray is through the written Word, His messengers such as prophets, and the personal direction of the Holy Ghost. Paul, as a mature believer and leader in the Body of Christ, would certainly have been able to hear and follow the voice of God without some sort of painful thorn. The whole idea that God placed the thorn in Paul's life is against the very nature of God as the giver of good gifts. It also contradicts the pattern by which He leads His children.

The next thing we must consider in determining the source of Paul's thorn is the text itself. Paul clearly told us that it was a messenger of Satan. Since it was Satan's messenger, why should we assume that it was sent by

God? In order to answer this question, some Bible students have turned to a couple passages from the Old Testament (I Kings 22, II Chronicles 18) where a lying spirit was sent to deceive King Ahab of Israel and King Jehoshaphat of Judah. However, careful examination of these incidents will reveal that these kings had already resisted the counsel and direction God had tried to give them; therefore, they – unlike Paul who was receiving and living by the revelations God had given him – were living in rebellion. Furthermore, it must be noted that the lying spirit actually asked God's permission to go and deceive the kings. Therefore, it was not a case of God's actually sending the evil spirit; rather, it was a case of His permitting it to go. A very similar scenario is played out in the life of King Saul in I Samuel 16:14. Since Paul's case does not parallel the cases of these rebellious kings of the Old Testament, we have no reason to try to equate the passages. The simplest way to interpret this passage is to read it as it is written – that Satan inflicted this thorn.

Having addressed the issue of the originator of the thorn, now we can go back the first question as to why it was sent. Seeing Satan as the originator of the thorn makes it readily obvious: it was sent to keep Paul from being exalted – or brought to a place of prominence in the church and world – because the Satanic kingdom suffered great losses every time Paul preached on the revelations he had been given. Even until today, the truths Paul brought to the Body of Christ are some of the most liberating principles ever taught. The devil desperately wanted to silence Paul. If he could keep people from receiving the apostle's message, he could keep them in his clutches! This thorn was not God's way of protecting Paul from pride, but Satan's way of trying to prevent Paul from gaining a place of advantage in his assault against the kingdom of darkness.

One other thing to remember would be that Paul has specifically addressed the issue of those in the Body who begin to feel self-important and inflated. In Romans 12:3, he warned them not to think more highly of themselves than they ought to think. If, indeed, Paul knew that this sort of self-exaltation would result in receiving a thorn in the flesh, isn't it likely that he would have incorporated a warning about such a result in this admonition about our personal evaluations of ourselves.

The next issue to consider would be the determination of the exact nature of Paul's thorn. Many teachers have proposed the notion that it was actually an eye disease. They, of course, draw upon the fact that Paul was blinded for three days at the time of his conversion on the road to Damascus. Added to this is Galatians 4:15 where Paul speaks of the fact that the people were so receptive to his ministry that they would have given him their eyeballs. Interpreting this statement to mean that he was having some sort of eye problem when he first preached in this city is just as erroneous as saying that an individual would have a paralyzed arm if someone was so willing to back him and his cause that he would use the expression, "I'll give you my right arm." Furthermore, such interpretations ignore the fact that Paul was healed of the blindness when Ananias laid hands on him and the fact that the Galatians passage does not specifically mention eye disease or blindness. Any conclusions drawn from this verse are based totally upon inferences and implications, not on specific factual information. However, we do have direct information and explanation concerning the nature of this thorn given in the text itself.

Paul says that his thorn was a messenger from Satan. The English term "messenger" is translated from the Greek word *aggelos* that can also be translated "angel." Paul recognized that his thorn was one of Satan's angels (Matthew 25:41, Revelation 12:9) that we know as demons. His thorn was not a physical ailment at all, but a demonic attack upon his person in general and his ministry in specific. It was Satan's attempt to keep him from being established in a place "above measure," or above the capacity of the devil's forces. By simply reading the story of Paul's life, we can easily see that he was harassed on every side by zealous Jewish opponents who considered him a heretic and wanted to stop his evangelistic work, by jealous Christians who mistrusted him or thought that his acceptance of the gentiles without their having to abide by the Jewish law was in violation of the faith, and even by the tempestuous forces of nature. In a passage in the preceding chapter Paul spoke – as he does in the passage we are studying – of the infirmities in which he is determined to glory. In this section, he gave a compilation of these obstacles that have been thrown across his path as he advanced the kingdom. (II Corinthians 11:23-28)

This dark cloud that seemed to be following Paul around was actually a demonic force that manifested itself through various avenues – sometimes through the forces of nature, sometimes through the Jewish religious leaders, and sometimes even through Paul's Christian brothers.

When Paul asked the Lord to remove this demonic attack, the heavens were silent on his first two requests. On the third approach, the Lord answered that the grace that Paul had already been given was sufficient for him to deal with the attack himself. God said that He didn't need to intervene because He had already made provision for Paul to deal with his adversary. In other words, God was telling Paul that he didn't need His present intervention since He had already made all the necessary provisions.

The Weapons of Our Warfare

In the last chapter, we made reference to the list of physical difficulties that Paul endured at the hands of his enemies and determined that God had already given the apostle the wherewithal to deal with them – divine grace. Notice how he introduces this enumeration of the attacks that had come against his life. He says that they were associated with his position as a minster of Christ.

> Are they ministers of Christ? (I speak as a fool) I am more; in labours more abundant, in stripes above measure, in prisons more frequent, in deaths oft. Of the Jews five times received I forty stripes save one. Thrice was I beaten with rods, once was I stoned, thrice I suffered shipwreck, a night and a day I have been in the deep; In journeyings often, in perils of waters, in perils of robbers, in perils by mine own countrymen, in perils by the heathen, in perils in the city, in perils in the wilderness, in perils in the sea, in perils among false brethren; In weariness and painfulness, in watchings often, in hunger and thirst, in fastings often, in cold and nakedness. Beside those things that are without, that which cometh upon me daily, the care of all the churches. (II Corinthian 11:23-28)

It is no coincidence that he introduces another significant listing in the same book with an almost identical comment.

> But in all things approving ourselves as the ministers of God, in much patience, in afflictions, in necessities, in distresses, In stripes, in imprisonments, in tumults, in

labours, in watchings, in fastings; By pureness, by knowledge, by long suffering, by kindness, by the Holy Ghost, by love unfeigned, By the word of truth, by the power of God, by the armour of righteousness on the right hand and on the left, By honour and dishonour, by evil report and good report: as deceivers, and yet true; As unknown, and yet well known; as dying, and, behold, we live; as chastened, and not killed; As sorrowful, yet alway rejoicing; as poor, yet making many rich; as having nothing, and yet possessing all things. (II Corinthians 6:4-10)

As we have already discussed in the analysis of the sword of the Spirit, the purposeful positioning of parallel words or thoughts in the scripture is a deliberate attempt to draw attention to the association between the two points. In this case, the apostle is showing us a list of the attacks that were levied against him and also giving us a list of the weapons that he used in confronting them. In the section in chapter six, Paul listed his persecutions as "in" in verses four and five. The ways he overcame them are listed as "by" in verses six, seven, and eight. The results of his defense are listed as "by" – a different preposition in Greek – in verses nine and ten. Interestingly, the approaches he used in his conflict are not the ones that we generally would list as our weapons for spiritual warfare; however, as we go through the explanations of these weapons, it will be obvious that they are simply manifestations of the grace of God working through the apostle. In the Living Bible, Ken Taylor translates II Corinthians 6:7 as, "All of the godly man's arsenal – weapons of defense, and weapons of attack – have been ours." Let's take a look at what is actually included in this arsenal of spiritual weapons.

First, he listed purity, the ability to keep a right heart attitude in the midst of conflict. The Old Testament character Joseph could serve as an excellent example. (Genesis 37:2-36, 39:1-50:25) His brothers plotted to kill him but decided that they could accomplish two things at once – get rid of their brother and make a little profit – by selling him into slavery. Thus they doomed him to a life of servitude in a less-than-human existence. Just when it looked as though his fortune was turning, his master's wife tried to entrap him and lied about the incident. His master never even gave Joseph a chance to defend himself but immediately threw into the dungeon. Years later, Joseph had an opportunity to get a fair trial, but the man who held his destiny in his hand forgot his promise and left Joseph languishing away in his cell. Eventually, Joseph was miraculously elevated to the place where he could have demanded the heads of all those who had perpetrated such injustices against him; however, he always kept the attitude that God meant for everything to come out for good in his life. Even when his brothers came begging for his mercy, he responded that he had nothing against them and promised to continue to take care of them and their children. Joseph went through hell with a heavenly attitude.

Next, Paul mentioned knowledge, knowing – not hoping or wishing – that God is on our side. Notice in each of the following scriptures from three different writers that each author tells us that his key is that he <u>knows</u> something:

> My brethren, count it all joy when ye fall into divers temptations; <u>Knowing</u> this, that the trying of your faith worketh patience. But let patience have her perfect work,

that ye may be perfect and entire, wanting nothing. (James 1:2-4)

For ye had compassion of me in my bonds, and took joyfully the spoiling of your goods, <u>knowing</u> in yourselves that ye have in heaven a better and an enduring substance. (Hebrews 10:34)

And not only so, but we glory in tribulations also: <u>knowing</u> that tribulation worketh patience; And patience, experience; and experience, hope: And hope maketh not ashamed; because the love of God is shed abroad in our hearts by the Holy Ghost which is given unto us. (Romans 5:3-5)

Paul's third entry is longsuffering. In Ephesians 4:2, Paul spoke of the purpose of longsuffering in the church – that of forbearing one another in love. Having already explained in Romans 2:4 and 9:22 that God manifests longsuffering for the purpose of bringing men to salvation, Paul now draws the logical conclusion that longsuffering in the Body of Christ is for the same purpose – to bring our fellow believers to their full salvation. By patiently working through their errors, immaturity, failures, and even deliberate rebellion, we lovingly hold them in the Body of Christ so that they can develop into strong believers. Paul demonstrated to us that longsuffering is not pampering the errant or enabling them to continue in their failures. His approach – that we would today label as "tough love" – may initially seem radical, but it actually mirrors the approach of our Heavenly Father who will allow the prodigal to go to the pigpen yet love him through the whole process. We see this sort of longsuffering in Paul's dealings with the Corinthian believers. It is amazing how much of his epistles to this congregation is dedicated to the waywardness of the church and the actual hostility that they developed against the apostle in the process. Yet, as Paul addressed and corrected them for their error and attitude, the underlying love that he had for them is evident in his longsuffering acceptance of them as his beloved – howbeit, rebellious – sons (I Corinthians 4:14-15) and the fact that he is perpetually thankful to God for them (I Corinthians 1:4). He point-blankly accused them of being contentious (I Corinthians 1:11), carnal rather than spiritual (I Corinthians 3:1), envious and full of strife (I Corinthians 3:3), and puffed up with pride (I Corinthians 4:18, 5:2). Additionally, he addressed their accusing attitude toward him and the low esteem in which they held him – one whom they could judge (I Corinthians 4:3), a fool while they were full of wisdom (I Corinthians 4:10), defamed, and filthy (I Corinthians 4:13). Paul also recorded their mocking response to his attempts to address their errant ways and attitudes – that he might be bold when writing letters but would cower in a face-to-face meeting. (I Corinthians 10:1, 10:10-11) Yet, he added that he purposely wanted to spare them any harsh face-to-face confrontation (I Corinthians 4:19-21, II Corinthians 2:1) and even apologized for disturbing them with his previous letter (II Corinthians 7:8). He went on to describe how that he had even sent his two most trusted assistants to help mediate the conflict. (I Corinthians 4:17, II Corinthians 7:6-7) Yet in all this effort to deal graciously with them, Paul was adamant that he would not renege on his position of their fault (I Corinthians 5:3) and that he would not back down on the necessity for the guilty ones to be dealt with (II Corinthians 13:2).

Kindness, helping even our enemies, is Paul's fourth item of weaponry. The Philippian jailer had beaten Paul and left him bound and bleeding while creepy, crawly things slithered across his back. Since his hands were tied, he could not defend himself from their invasion and infection. Yet, when the jailer was ready to commit hari-kari, Paul rushed to his rescue and saved his life – and then his soul. (Acts 16:22-34)   I've often wondered how long I might have hesitated in calling out to the jailer were I in Paul's place. My guess is that I would likely have paused just long enough for the man to inflict an irreversible injury. Paul, however, was so full of kindness that he simply couldn't stand to see the jailer – no matter how cruel he had been – suffer injury and death.

Paul calls his next entry simply the Holy Ghost. I'm certain that he meant to imply the entire influence of the Spirit in a Christian's life – the fruit of the Spirit (Galatians 5:22-23), living in the Spirit (Galatians 5:25), walking in the Spirit (Galatians 5:16), being spiritually minded (Romans 8:6), and being led by the Spirit so as to not fulfill the lusts of the flesh (Galatians 5:18).

The reason that we want to lash out and defend ourselves against evil is that we are not totally led by the Holy Spirit. If we were, we would constantly be aware that hurt people hurt people. The result would be that we would be more like Jesus Himself who even prayed for His executioners – knowing that what they were doing was beyond their own knowledge. (Luke 23:34)   The real impact of this verse doesn't appear in the English version of the Bible in that the continuous nature of the Greek verb isn't translated.   It seems that Luke was trying to communicate that – throughout the entire ordeal – Jesus was crying out for the forgiveness of those who were so hostilely abusing Him. With each mocking jeer, with each mouthful of spit, with every fistful of beard that was plucked out, with each lash of the whip, with each thorn in His brow, with each pounding of the nail the corridors of heaven echoed with the earnest intercession of the Lord, "Father, forgive! They have no idea what they are doing!" We must also remember that Jesus taught us that unforgiveness would actually negate all our prayers (Mark 11:25) – an often overlooked aspect of the popular teaching about faith and positive confession based on the two preceding verses.

When the Holy Spirit does His revelatory work inside of us, we'll understand that the animosity that people exhibit toward us is only a manifestation of the turmoil that is raging inside their own souls.

Love unfeigned – or as the New King James Version says "sincere love" – might seem to be a strange implement for warfare, but it appears prominently as the next entry on Paul's list. In the New Testament time, most upper class families displayed marble statues in their homes and yards. If these marble statues were chipped or cracked, they were often patched with wax. In the statuary shops, the flawless items were marked as being *sine cera (*without wax). Paul's weapon – and ours – is flawless and genuine love, with no façade, which prepares us to become overcomers in our times of struggle.

> Whosoever believeth that Jesus is the Christ is born of God: and every one that loveth him that begat loveth him also that is begotten of him. By this we know that we love the children of God, when we love God, and keep his commandments. For this is the love of God, that we keep his commandments: and his commandments are not grievous. For whatsoever is born of God overcometh the world: and this is the victory that overcometh the world, even our faith. (I John 5:1-4)

Jesus really raised the bar on the idea of love unfeigned when He told us that we were to love our enemies. (Matthew 5:44; Luke 6:27, 35) This kind of behavior is so against the human nature that if it doesn't draw our enemies to the Christ inside us, it will drive them crazy trying to figure out what's happening. Seriously, history is full of testimonies of Christians who – even when facing martyrdom – used this weapon of unfeigned love on their executioners and won them to Christ. Many of the stories have follow-up chapters of the faith of those who came to Christ through the love of those whom they were persecuting. Many even wound up joining them on the chopping block or at the fiery stake to give their own lives for the Lord.

The word of truth appears next. Here Paul contrasted Satan's strongholds of deception that he mentioned in chapter ten verses three through five against the positive mind of God that he talked about in chapter four verses sixteen through eighteen. Satan's thoughts are actually lies that make us slaves; God's thoughts are truths that set us free. Paul had determined to focus on the liberating thoughts of God's truth. Paul's focus was on the streets of gold, not the stones hitting him in the head; the loving embrace of Jesus, not the strong arm of the Roman beating him; his eternal home, not the present tribulation. He was so focused on the heaven he was going to that he barely noticed the hell he was going through.

When Paul added the power of God to his armament belt, I believe that he was talking about God's constructive – not destructive – power. Even though he was writing about warfare, I doubt that he was like James and John – the Sons of Thunder – who wanted to call down heavenly fire upon their opponents when Jesus replied that they did not know what spirit they were of. (Luke 9:54-55) I believe that he was praying exactly as the first church did when they encountered their initial persecution. In

Acts 4:29-30, when the church prayed after the first confrontation, they did not ask God to "get" their enemies! Rather, they asked God to continue to stretch forth His hand and heal through them. Let's be honest – how often do we react like the Sons of Thunder rather than the Sons of God?

In essence, Paul is telling us that his way of dealing with the attacks of the enemy was to simply employ the instructions of Jesus Himself:

> But I say unto you, Love your enemies, bless them that curse you, do good to them that hate you, and pray for them which despitefully use you, and persecute you. (Matthew 5:44)
>
> But I say unto you which hear, Love your enemies, do good to them which hate you. (Luke 6:27)
>
> But love ye your enemies, and do good, and lend, hoping for nothing again; and your reward shall be great, and ye shall be the children of the Highest: for he is kind unto the unthankful and to the evil. (Luke 6:35)

This was a message that Paul himself endorsed and promoted in his own writings:

> Be not overcome of evil, but overcome evil with good. (Romans 12:21)
>
> See that none render evil for evil unto any man; but ever follow that which is good, both among yourselves, and to all men. (I Thessalonians 5:15)

Many contemporary translations actually try incorporate the idea that Paul's weapons were actually his righteous deeds through which he confronted and overcome evil with good: "weapons of righteousness"

(Amplified), "righteous weapons" (Complete Jewish Bible), "In all our struggles we have said and done only what is right" (Contemporary English Version), "arms of righteousness" (Darby's Translation), "weapons of righteousness" (Disciples Literal New Testament), "this right way of living" (Easy to Read Version), "right living with weapons of righteousness" (Expanded Bible), "We have righteousness as our weapon" (Good News Translation), "We use our right living to defend ourselves against everything" (Children's Bible), "Our sole defense, our only weapon, is a life of integrity" (Phillips Translation), "Our right living to defend ourselves against everything" (New Century Version), "weapons of godliness" (New International Reader's Version), "the sword of being right with God" (New Life Version), "armed on the right and armed on the left with righteousness from God" (The Voice), and "These are the right things to use in our fight" (Worldwide English).

The conclusion that Paul comes to in verses nine and ten is that even though he described himself as suffering serious blows, he always seemed to bounce back victoriously. He was like the good man described in Proverbs 24:16 who, even if he falls seven times, always gets up again. The roly-poly toys we know as weebles can help us understand the powerful spiritual truth that dominated Paul's life. We've all enjoyed the amazement of "socking" the punch toy as hard as we can and watching it plop all the way to the floor – only to immediately bounce back totally erect.

Another side note to this passage is that Paul described having the weaponry in each hand. It seems that the significance of this concept might go back to the time of the rebuilding of the wall around Jerusalem under Nehemiah's direction. In Nehemiah 4:17, we read, "They which builded on the wall, and they that bare burdens, with those that laded, every one with one of his hands wrought in the work, and with the other hand held a weapon." These were two-fisted warriors who were slapping mortar on the blocks with a trowel in one hand and threatening their enemies with a sword with the other. Building the wall was a passive form of defense while yielding a sword was an active form of defense. In this approach, we see a great lesson for all believers – build yourself up in your faith as a passive resistance to the enemy's attacks while also aggressively challenging him every time he shows up!

At this point, you might be asking the same question that one of my students once challenged me with, "So how do you consider Paul more than a conqueror when he was enduring beatings, prison, shipwrecks, and stoning?" My answer is to turn to yet another passage in the same epistle, "For our light affliction, which is but for a moment, worketh for us a far more exceeding and eternal weight of glory." (II Corinthians 4:17) So what is the connection between the afflictions and the glory that was to be revealed. In exactly the same way that Satan totally misjudged the crucifixion, thinking that it would be the end of Jesus rather than the beginning of His dominion (I Corinthians 2:8), he didn't see that his attacks on the apostle would actually perpetuate his ministry into the millennia. Obviously, the devil didn't realize that by putting Paul in prison he was simply giving him the free time to write the epistles that have changed countless millions of lives over the ensuing twenty centuries. (II Timothy 2:9) Nor did he realize that instigating others to try to slander the apostle simply accentuated his ministry. (Philippians 1:12-18) Similarly, he didn't seem to comprehend that his chains were not a source of shame (II Timothy 1:8, 1:16) but were actually an avenue for the fulfillment of the ministry that had been prophetically spoken over Paul from the day of his conversion (Acts 9:15-16). For certain, he didn't foresee that all his schemes would actually set the stage for the gospel to penetrate right into Caesar's own household – the most powerful circle of influence in the world! (Philippians 4:22) In the divine irony that followed the pattern of Haman erecting his own gallows (Esther 7:10), the man digging the very pit that he would later fall into (Proverbs 26:27), and Daniel's enemies finding themselves in the lion's den that they planned for the prophet (Daniel 6:24), everything that the devil planned against the apostle "backfired in his own face"! The afflictions that the devil perpetrated against the apostle paved the way for a glorious furtherance of the gospel.

As I have already mentioned, my summation of Paul's evaluation of his "light afflictions" is that the apostle was so focused on the heaven that he was going <u>to</u> that he barely noticed the hell that he was going <u>through</u>. Paul had won a much bigger battle than the struggle against the external attacks upon him. He had won the war against the internal struggle within himself that would have made him <u>react</u> to the way the enemy would <u>abuse</u> him rather than to <u>respond</u> to the way the Lord would <u>use</u> him through these situations. (Acts 9:15-16) Jesus expressed it this way, "A woman when she is in travail hath sorrow, because her hour is come: but as soon as she is delivered of the child, she remembereth no more the anguish, for joy that a man is born into the world." (John 16:21) We all know women who go through the birthing process multiple times because their focus is on the long-term joy of raising a family rather than on the short-term pain of the delivery. This thought brings us to one more passage from the book of II Corinthians – a section of scripture which specifically speaks of the weapons of our spiritual warfare.

> For though we walk in the flesh, we do not war after the flesh: (For the weapons of

our warfare are not carnal, but mighty through God to the pulling down of strong holds;) Casting down imaginations, and every high thing that exalteth itself against the knowledge of God, and bringing into captivity every thought to the obedience of Christ. (II Corinthians 10:3-5)

Notice the mention of strongholds, imaginations, and thoughts in these verses. To get a grasp on what these terms mean, we need to take a short time travel journey back to the time of King David. When David set out on his campaign to take the city of Jerusalem, the Jebusites boasted that he need not even try in that the city was a stronghold and that it was so secure that its guards were the blind and the lame men. (II Samuel 5:6) Its natural position made it virtually impenetrable; therefore, it was unnecessary to position the able-bodied soldiers there. These strong warriors were used elsewhere while the disabled veterans defended the city. The city actually defended itself since it was built on the top of high cliffs with deep ravines surrounding it. When under attack, all these physically-challenged soldiers had to do was to simply push boulders over the edge of the cliff upon the approaching forces. They did not need to be marksmen or skilled warriors.

After David took the city, Jerusalem then became his stronghold. (II Samuel 5:7-9) From the city of Jerusalem, we learn a lesson concerning strongholds: their power is in their natural position. You don't have to have a strong warrior inside a stronghold to be able to protect it because the stronghold itself is its own protection. Let's apply this principle to our own lives – specifically our thought lives. The devil doesn't have to be strong to have a powerful control over us. He could use lame ideas and blind assumptions to exercise tremendous authority. He doesn't have to have real strength or ability as long as he has a controlling position in our thought life. When the devil gets inside our thinking and begins to feed us with lies and deception, he saps whatever energy and power was already inside us.

On the other hand, the truth can get inside our stronghold and make it just as strong a fortification for the truth as it was for the devil's lies.

The power of our mind is incredible. When we believe the devil's thoughts of defeat, we are defeated. When the thoughts of God get into our minds and our spirits and fill us with thoughts of success, we are successful. Just as David transformed the city of the Jebusites into his prized capital, Jesus is intent upon taking the strongholds of Satan and making them His treasured show places. One interesting aspect to the story of David's conquest of the city is that he armed it with his mighty men – not the lame and blind men as did the Jebusites. In like fashion, when Christ takes over our minds and hearts, He fortifies our strongholds with the powerful truths of the Word of God! The verb translated "keep" in Philippians 4:7 literally means to build a fort. In Christ, we can fortify our minds with powerful truths that declare and determine victory.

For many years when I read the passage about our spiritual weapons and how they take authority over our vain imaginations and thought that exalt themselves against the knowledge of God, I thought that these were things like atheism that says there is no God. I thought that Paul was saying that the weapons of my warfare were for the purpose of destroying the arguments of the people who say there is no God. In actuality, this is not at all what this passage is saying. Our weapons are strong enough to destroy all the arguments against any area of the knowledge about God. There are lots of things that we should know about God; however, for some reason, we don't because there is an idea that has gotten into our heads that keeps the true knowledge of God from getting into us. We know that God exists, but we fail to attain the true knowledge of who God is and what God does. God is Jehovah Tsidkenu, which means that He is the God of our righteousness. The day that Jesus came into our lives, His righteousness came into us. However, the devil will come to each of us with accusations to combat our righteousness consciousness. If that lie penetrates into our minds and we agree with it, he begins to build a stronghold against the knowledge of God's righteousness within us. God is also Jehovah Rapha – the God who heals all of our diseases – but the devil wants to plant lies inside us saying that our ailment is either too big for God to heal or too insignificant for Him to notice. The truth is that God is just as willing to heal the little aches and pains as He is willing to heal cancer. He is just as able to heal the most dreaded plague, as He is able to cure a minor ailment. We can go through all the redemptive names and qualities of God to learn what we should be thinking about God. Any time we allow thoughts contrary to these truths into our hearts, we have permitted the enemy to use his deceit to begin a stronghold in our minds.

    One of the unique characteristics of strongholds is that they are positioned so that in the event of an attack, enemies would actually bring destruction upon themselves. In Sri Lanka, I have climbed to the top of Sigiriya, the spectacular "Lion Rock" fortress on top a gigantic rock whose sheer walls rise about twelve hundred feet above its luscious green jungle surroundings. This fortress, built in AD 473, was surrounded by huge slaps of stone that were triggered with rope mechanisms so that an avalanche of destruction would instantly engulf any intruding army. In Israel, I was able to climb the equally impressive fortress of Masada that was built by King Herod. This encampment poised atop the thirteen-hundred-foot precipice became the last bastion of the Jewish people against the Roman invasion. When the legion laid siege to the fortress in AD 72, the Romans realized that the only way to take the stronghold was to build a circumvallation wall to allow them to approach the plateau. They forced Jewish slaves to haul in the thousands of tons of stones and earth that it took to build the ramp because the attackers knew that the Jews in the fortress would not kill their national brethren. Otherwise, the Jews hold-up in the fortress would have pummeled their attackers to death with their arsenal of rocks. From my vantage point perched atop Sigiriya or Masada, thinking of the sheer insanity of launching an attack against either of these strongholds, I began to gain a perspective of how well defensible our position in Christ can and should be if we only renew our minds to become strongholds of truth rather than citadels for the enemy's blind assumptions and lame ideas.

Let's examine how David outsmarted the Jebusites when he took the city of Jerusalem from the lame and blind guards. According to II Samuel 5:8, his tactical approach was through the water canal. In Ephesians 5:26, Paul uses water as a symbol of the Word of God. If this symbol can also be applied to the story of David's conquest of Jerusalem, we can see that the lesson exactly parallels biblical truth – the only way we are to take control of the strongholds in our lives is to infiltrate them with the truth of the Word of God – the weapon that is more powerful than the enemy's lies. One interesting footnote to this story is that the King James translation of this verse says that he sent his men into the city through the gutter. What a powerful thought – what had been a gutter, filled with the garbage thoughts of this world, became the avenue through which the renewing and life-giving truths of God could invade! Perhaps that is the reason David wrote that he had hidden the Word of God in his heart so that he would not sin against God (Psalm 119:11) and prayed that the Lord would search his heart to see if there was any evil way in it (Psalm 139:23). His son Solomon followed with his own admonition concerning the importance of the heart when he said in Proverbs 4:23, "Keep (guard) thy heart with all diligence; for out of it are the issues of life." In Psalm 19:14 we find a powerful key, "Let the words of my mouth, and the meditation of my heart, be acceptable in thy sight, O LORD, my strength, and my redeemer." David prayed that the words of his mouth – the sayings he initiated and the things that he repeated from others – would be acceptable unto the Lord. Let me suggest that David likely used the same filter that is described in the New Testament as a screen for eliminating words and thoughts that would have been displeasing to God:

> Finally, brethren, whatsoever things are true, whatsoever things are honest, whatsoever things are just, whatsoever things are pure, whatsoever things are lovely, whatsoever things are of good report; if there be any virtue, and if there be any praise, think on these things. (Philippians 4:8)

Here Paul listed eight criteria that must be met before any thought qualifies to be meditated upon. Simply being true does not make it eligible to become part of our thinking process. Once it passes the truth filter, it then must be subjected to the filter of justice and the honesty filter, followed by the purity filter, then the filter of loveliness, the good-report filter, the virtue filter, and the praiseworthiness filter. If it makes it through all these filters, then – and only then – is it acceptable for a Christian to think or meditate on.

So what does this say about the bad news reports that we hear? How should they affect us? First of all, we need to determine if they are true. Quite simply, much of what is published today – even in many reputable news sources – simply is not true. In that case, ignore it unless you have an opportunity to correct the misinformation in order to protect other innocent subjects. Next, we must apply the just and honest filters to determine if what is said is presented with a bias that is distorting the truth. The kernel of truth that inspired the gossip may be true, but what about the assumptions or exaggerations that came along with it? An old expression goes, "Figures don't lie, but liars figure." For example, all of the scientific evidences that have been presented as proof of evolution actually have another story to tell – one that proves the instantaneous creation of the universe by an intelligent being. However, the scientific publications as a whole are unjust and dishonest in the way they report this information. Since the reports have failed the next layers of filters, we have to discard them from our meditations unless we have the ability to correct the interpretations into honest and just concepts. Other filters include purity, loveliness, praiseworthiness, and virtue. These filters readily disqualify any kinds of reports that slander and harm others. Obviously, when people are in error, they need to be corrected; but slander or "getting even" are not correction! Therefore, we must not meditate on these aspects of the issue. Rather, we must meditate on a positive quality associated with their wrongdoing – the fact that Jesus came to redeem fallen men and that He gave us the ministry of reconciling these wayward men to Him.

One other test is the good-report filter where we have to ask ourselves if the report is good as well as true. If what we hear is true but negative in nature, it does not qualify as a tenant for space in our hearts and minds. That doesn't mean that we ignore the truth; it simply means that we are not to meditate on it. In an economic downturn, for an example, it would be foolish to ignore the fact that the economy is in serious difficulty; however, to allow that negative report to become a focal point in our thoughts would be disastrous. Instead, we can focus on another report that is true but also passes the good-report test, "But my God shall supply all your need according to his riches in glory by Christ Jesus." (Philippians 4:19)

The conclusion of the struggle seems to be that God has already given us the grace to win and put us into the position of victory; our only challenge is to get our knowledge and faith to the full level. Perhaps this is what the author of the book of Hebrews was referencing when he spoke of laboring in order to come into rest and ensuring that we don't fail through unbelief. (Hebrews 4:11) Additionally, we should also recognize that the scriptures repeatedly testify that our fight is not necessarily against demonic forces but in the arena of our faith. (I Timothy 6:12, II Timothy 4:7-8, Jude 3) Furthermore, we must realize – as the author of Hebrews confirms – that if the battle is lost, it will be in our minds. (Hebrews 12:3) But the final word on the matter is jubilant, "This is the victory that overcometh the world, even our faith." (I John 5:4)

The Ultimate Example

We have just one more biblical account to "unpack" – the ultimate example of a spiritual struggle. However, before we go there, it would be good for us to take a few minutes to recap and analyze the stories we have already examined.

We opened our study with a narrative about my experience in the dorm parking lot close to half a century ago. The lesson that we took away from that event was that my struggle was caused by a misconception about how I was to relate to God and the world that I lived in. Because I had been taught that living the Christian life was an "uphill" struggle, I felt that there must be something wrong with me when I didn't see every day as a battle to keep the faith. It was only through my relationship with my parents that mirrored the relationship that God wanted me to have with Him that I was able to overcome all the misconceptions and fears that hassled me.

We also spent a few paragraphs looking at the concept of travailing in prayer. Using Paul's request in Romans 15:30-32 that his Christian brothers and sisters contend with him in prayer, we questioned exactly what battle it was that necessitated their assistance. Placing the request in the historical context of Paul's life, it seems that the issue was not the challenges that the enemy was to throw at him; rather, his trial would be facing the well-meaning Christians who would try to dissuade him from continuing his journey to Jerusalem once the Holy Spirit revealed the danger that lurked there. In the face of all his good-intentioned advisors, Paul insisted that he was not going to alter his course because the Holy Spirit had directed him to take each step in faith. The moral of this story is that our struggles may not be against the enemy's overt attacks but against innocent-looking diversions from the will of God – some of which might even come through friends and Christian brothers and sisters.

Jacob's wrestling match with the angel taught an important point – many of our struggles are totally pointless. Even after blessings had been repeatedly spoken over him and God had clearly directed him to return to the land of his father, Jacob still felt that he had to accomplish his goals through his own human conniving and that he had to struggle in order to gain a blessing. Obviously, his whole life could have been much simpler and less stressful if only he had decided to receive rather than to wrestle for the favor of God and man.

The episode in Esther's life when she called for a three-day fast helped us understand the necessity of afflicting the soul – our mental processes, emotional motivations, and willful desires – in order to get to that place of submission where our bodies and souls are yielded to our spirits so that it is easy to walk according to the will of God as it is dictated to us by the Holy Spirit's speaking to our human spirits.

The story of the disciples' failed attempt to set the demon-possessed boy free highlighted the necessity to live a lifestyle of fasting and prayer in order to eliminate unbelief and doubt from our lives. It seems fairly apparent in the story that the demon inside the boy was not nearly as big a challenge to Jesus as the unbelief inside his father and the faithlessness inside the disciples.

Paul's discussion of the armor of God brought up the all-important point that we should live in a position of authority so that we don't ever have to worry about wrestling with principalities. When we understand who we are in Christ and who He is inside of us, we stand resiliently against the devil without having to abdicate our position as <u>more</u> than conquerors in order to wrestle with him to obtain the position of conquerors.

In the tale of Jehoshaphat's simultaneous confrontation with multiple enemies, we saw a clear illustration of some important lessons. Before he made a move, the king sought the Lord and dug into His Word in order to confirm within himself exactly what promises from God were applicable to his present situation. Once he had a grasp on the appropriate covenant provisions, he called the people together and had them recommit themselves to the promises of God and the God of the promises. At that point, he realized that he was already on the winning side of the war and could celebrate his victory even before engaging in a battle.

Paul's discussion of the thorn in his flesh gave us some important insight into our direct confrontations with messengers of Satan. Originally, Paul wanted God to do something to help him. The answer came back that God did not need to intervene for Paul; instead, He had already provided everything that the apostle needed – His grace. Paul's real problem wasn't the attack of the enemy but his need to be aware of what God had already given him and to appropriate and activate that provision. By laying claim to and demonstrating the grace of God, Paul was able to manifest the authority that he had as more than a conqueror by overcoming evil with good.

The stories of the gentleman who went to his friend to ask for bread and the widow who insisted that the unjust judge rule favorably in her behalf both challenge us to rethink our perception of how willing God is to answer our prayers. When we come to the unquestionable conviction that He is more desirous to bless us than we are to be blessed, we'll no longer feel the necessity to pray grueling prayers of petition trying to earn His benefits by our own arguments, eloquently framed prayers, or emotionally-charged persistence. Oh, that we could all get that same revelation that came to me on that night in the front seat of my little burgundy Mustang – that God wants us to relate to Him as a loving, gracious, sacrificing father rather than a grumpy neighbor or disinterested judge.

Daniel's twenty-one days of intercession teach two simple lessons. The first is the same axiom that the Lord explained to Jehoshaphat – the battle is the Lord's, not ours. The second is that the battle is actually already over now that Jesus has put Satan under <u>His</u> feet (Genesis 3:15) and has determined that He will soon put him under <u>our</u> feet as well. (Romans 16:20).

However, the greatest of all episodes of spiritual struggle awaits our attention – the story of Jesus' agonizing struggle in the Garden of Gethsemane. Before we go there, we must take a short detour through the desert of temptation. But even before we can get to that desert, we must make one preliminary stopover at the River Jordan to observe the events of Jesus' baptism by John. Each of the synoptic gospel accounts confirm that God spoke audibly, pronouncing that Jesus as His Beloved Son. (Matthew 3:17, Mark 1:11, Luke 3:22) It was immediately after this supernatural display of divine affirmation that Jesus went into the desert for the forty days of fasting and the dramatic confrontation with the devil. The significant issue that Satan repeatedly challenged Jesus with in the temptation was based totally on trying to get Jesus to question the relationship that God has just confirmed. (Matthew 4:3, 4:6; Luke 4:3, 4:9) No matter how much the devil pushed the issue, Jesus was unwavering in the temptation because He was fully convinced of His divine sonship and was not dissuaded even with misconstrued Bible quotations. He always answered with the Word of God in proper context – the sword of the Spirit as we already know. (Ephesians 6:17)

Before we examine the three-hour struggle in the Garden of Gethsemane, we must realize one important truth – this battle was not a confrontation with the devil. During the dialogue that Jesus had with His disciples at the Last Supper just prior to going to the garden, He declared that the devil was about to make his major power play of all history but he had nothing inside of Jesus Himself. (John 14:30) Therefore, the inner contention that was about to play out in Gethsemane was not between Jesus and the devil but between two factions within the Master Himself.

There seems to be one common denominator between the temptation in the desert and this agonizing experience that led up to the arrest and crucifixion – the word, "If." In the desert, Satan continually questioned if Jesus was the Son of God; in the garden, Jesus questioned if there was some other way for Him to fulfill His mission. (Matthew 26:39, 26:42; Mark 14:35) This is an amazing turn of events in that Jesus Himself had actually repeatedly prophesied about His death (Matthew 16:21–28, 17:22–23, 20:17–19, 26:26-28; Mark 8:31–33, 9:30–32, 14:22–24; Luke 9:22–27, 22:19-20; John 12:7, 12:23, 12:32); therefore, He knew the Father's plan and will prior to entering into the agonizing prayer.

The author of the epistle to the Hebrews described the struggle, making it even more poignant by contrasting the prayers of Jesus with the Old Testament prophecies, showing that Jesus had unquestionable assurance even though He was going through this torturous ordeal.

> So also Christ glorified not himself to be made an high priest; but he that said unto him, Thou art my Son, to day have I begotten thee. As he saith also in another place, Thou art a priest for ever after the order of Melchisedec. Who in the days of his flesh, when he had offered up prayers and supplications with strong crying and

tears unto him that was able to save him from death, and was heard in that he feared. (Hebrews 5:5-7)

There are two little words in the concluding phrases of this passage that are strategic – "heard" and "feared." Let's look at the second one first. The idea of fear draws us into the humanity of Jesus that was manifest as He faced the crucifixion. The other point of interest here is the fact that He was heard by the One who was able to save Him – God. In light of the fact that I John 5:14-15 teaches us that we can have confidence that God hears our prayers when they are prayed in accordance to His will, we must question how this agonizing prayer was answered. Since the Father only really pays attention to prayers that are prayed in His will, it seems that Jesus' prayers must have been in the will of God. After all, that was the very foundation of His teaching on prayer – that we should pray for God's will to be accomplished on earth in the exact manner in which it is fulfilled in heaven. (Matthew 6:10) When Jesus repeatedly pleaded for there to be an alternative to the set plan, was this an indication that He was out of the will of God? No, it simply points out that there was a struggle between His spirit man and His fleshly man. Throughout the struggle, the spirit man was willing and submitted even though the fleshly man was fearful and weak. (Matthew 26:41) The Father was always hearing and answering the cry of the spirit, but the manifestation of His answer was delayed by the weakness of Jesus' flesh.

When Jesus finally got His human nature to submit to His divine nature, there was no longer a struggle. He did not resist in the arrest. In fact, one interesting turn of events was the encounter between Peter and Malchus. Peter, wanting to become a conqueror, drew his sword and cut of the man's ear – likely proving that he was not very skilled with a sword in that he was probably aiming for the man's throat. (Luke 22:49) Jesus, on the other hand, knew that He was now submitted to the Father's will that would make Him the Conqueror through the cross and resurrection. Therefore, He reached down and healed the Malchus' ear in spite of – or possibly, because of – the fact that the soldier was there to arrest Him. Jesus didn't defend Himself during the trial and didn't resist during the flogging and crucifixion. When the devil motivated bystanders to try the same approach that had failed him in the desert – to question if Jesus were certain that He were the Son of God – there was no wavering. (Matthew 27:40) Interestingly, the action that they challenged Him with was to come down from the cross – a very tempting solution to two questions that He had already settled. Coming down from the cross would necessitate another way to fulfill His mission – the prayer He had struggled with in Gethsemane. It would have also demonstrated His supernatural ability – verifying that He was some sort of superhuman entity and very likely the Son of God. Yet Jesus did not succumb to the temptation because He had already dealt with His weak and fearful flesh in the garden.

The significance of this dramatic story is that it validates all our struggles. If Jesus Himself had to go through such agonizing struggles, we need not be ashamed or discouraged when we find ourselves torn and agonizing.

> For we have not an high priest which cannot be touched with the feeling of our infirmities; but was in all points tempted like as we are, yet without sin. (Hebrews 4:15)

The thing that we have to remember, however, is that once we successfully contend with our inner doubts, fears, and lack of faith and get our knowledge and faith levels up to the level of the grace that God has already set in motion inside of us, we'll be able to stand unflinchingly against any assaults that the world, the flesh, or the devil try to mount against us. At this point, I'm reminded of a motto that is posted on the local fitness center wall, "It's our own minds that we need to convince that we can do this." Armed with this awareness, we can turn our eyes toward the eastern sky and – as Jacob of old – see that there is a new dawn rising and that our struggle is over!

> We have also a more sure word of prophecy; whereunto ye do well that ye take heed, as unto a light that shineth in a dark place, until the day dawn, and the day star arise in your hearts: (II Peter 1:19)
>
> I Jesus have sent mine angel to testify unto you these things in the churches. I am the root and the offspring of David, and the bright and morning star. (Revelation 22:16) To give knowledge of salvation unto his people by the remission of their sins, Through the tender mercy of our God; whereby the dayspring from on high hath visited us, To give light to them that sit in darkness and in the shadow of death, to guide our feet into the way of peace. (Luke 1:77-79)
>
> But unto you that fear my name shall the Sun of righteousness arise with healing in his wings. (Malachi 4:2)

Teach All Nations Mission

Teach All Nations Mission (TAN) is a global evangelical educational ministry birthed from the teaching ministries of Delron and Peggy Shirley. The name for Teach All Nations Mission was chosen to carefully indicate the exact heart of the Shirleys' mission. TAN's commitment is to establish a solid biblical foundation in national pastors and leaders so they can help enrich their own people. This vision is being accomplished by holding national leadership conferences and publishing and distributing Christian teaching materials in English and their local languages.

Someone accurately observed concerning the revival that is occurring in many parts of our world today that it is a mile wide but only an inch deep – the result of energetic evangelism by both missionaries and local Christians. Sadly, there is a marked shortage of teachers who are taking the next step in fulfilling our Lord's directive to teach them how to observe all that He has commanded. Therefore, Teach All Nations Mission has literally taken the words of Christ from Matthew 28:19, "Teach all nations," as its motto and mission statement.

TAN's commitment is to deepen that revival by training the pastors and leaders who then go back and strengthen their congregations. TAN pays for the travel and lodging of handpicked leaders because Delron and Peggy want to invest into their lives but know that these third-world saints could never afford to come at their own expense. TAN always provides the meals for all the guests during these conferences. The ministry also furnishes solid Christian literature in their local language or in English for those who understand the language.

Delron and Peggy realize that the challenge is much bigger than what they can accomplish in person; therefore, they have determined to expand the scope of their vision.

One area of expansion includes a scholarship fund that will allow selected individuals to obtain a formal education in solid Christian colleges and Bible schools or through correspondence courses. The ministry has also assisted in building a Christian school in Zimbabwe and a Bible college in Nepal. Additionally, Teach All Nations assists the pastors and leaders they work with in times of need such as the tsunami in Sri Lanka, the earthquake in Nepal, and hurricanes in Belize and in the Turks and Caicos Islands.

    Your gifts to and prayers for Teach All Nations will help the Shirleys continue their outreach to Christian leadership around the world.

Teach All Nations Mission
3210 Cathedral Spires
Colorado Springs, CO 8904
719-685-9999
www.teachallnationsmission.com
teachallnations@msn.com

**Books by Delron & Peggy Shirley
available at www.teachallnationsmission.com**

Bingo, a Fresh Look at Grace
Christmas Thoughts
Cornerstones of Faith
Daily Bible Study Series (Five-Volume Set)
Daily Ditties from Delron's Desk (Six Volumes Available)
Dr. Livingstone, I Presume
The Great Commission – Doable
Finally, My Brethren
Going Deeper in Jesus
In This Sign Conquer
Interface
Israel, Key to Human Destiny
Lessons Along the Way
Lessons from the Life of David
Living for the End Times
Maturing into the Full Stature of Jesus Christ
Maximum Impact
Of Kings and Prophets
Passion for the Harvest
People Who Make A Difference
Positioned for Blessing and Power
Problem People of the Bible
Seeds and Harvest
So, You Wanna be a Preacher
The IN Factors
The Last Enemy
The Non-Conformer's Trilogy
Tread Marks
Verse for the Day (Two Volumes Available)
Women for the Harvest
You'll be Darned to Heck if You Don't Believe in Gosh
Your Home Can Survive in the 21st Century

www.ingramcontent.com/pod-product-compliance
Lightning Source LLC
LaVergne TN
LVHW021400080426
835508LV00020B/2383